Future Mommy

The Ultimate Guide for First Time Moms

Yesenia Mooring

from various sources. Please consult a licensed professional before attempting any techniques outlined in this book.

By reading this document, the reader agrees that under no circumstances is the author responsible for any losses, direct or indirect, that are incurred as a result of the use of the information contained within this document, including, but not limited to, errors, omissions, or inaccuracies.

Table of Contents

Introduction

"You're always going to wonder if you're doing things wrong, but that's what it means to be a mom, to care so much about someone else that you just want to be as perfect as possible." — Naya Rivera

Motherhood is full of so many gifts to look forward to. As you approach the role for the very first time, there can be a lot of overwhelming obstacles to face. If you are wondering if you have what it takes, this book will help you realize that you are capable of being a wonderful mother. Through the wisdom that is shared, you will find yourself feeling inspired and confident in the skills that you have. With the nurturing energy that you already possess, you will learn how to use it to parent your child successfully and healthily.

According to research, the most successful mothers are the following:

- Happy
- Role Models
- Engaged
- Focused

Information was gathered from 13,000 couples in the UK by the University of London. These couples all had one thing in common—they had children born in 2000 or 2001. When the child was nine months old, the researchers surveyed the parents' happiness. In another 14 years, the same survey was taken. The results found that if the mother was happy, the child was happier. With the health of the couple, the mother being happy also influenced if they were still together or not. This shows how important it is to establish a sense of happiness as you approach motherhood. Find what makes you feel great.

Reading this book before your baby arrives is a perfect time. This gives you the chance to practice the advice and tips given. Before you know it, they will become second-nature to you. It is typical to worry about motherhood, even if you are super excited to meet your baby. Some common worries range from wondering if you can protect your kids from harm to making the wrong choices.

"I worry about her getting sick a lot, I worry about SIDS, I worry that she won't have friends when she's older, I literally worry about everything." — Diana M., mother

You are going to be filled with worry sometimes, that is part of being a great mom! What matters most is that you do not let these worries take control. Instead, you will learn how to combat them by providing yourself with reassurance. For some things, they can only be practiced with a hands-on approach. A lot of motherhood is going to be this way. You can read plenty of books, but when it comes down to it, you will be relying on your maternal instincts a lot. Having a good combination of factual information and instincts is going to be your key to success.

Despite all of the information available to use as resources, many mothers still feel alone. Not to mention, there are other mothers all around you who are feeling the same way. Millennial Moms surveyed a group of mothers in 2018 and found that 85% of them do not feel supported by society. It can be a tough job, especially with a lack of support! Through the help of this book, you will learn how to both support yourself and find others who are going to provide you with emotional support. If you have a partner in your life, you will also learn how to rely on them more, trusting that they can give you what you need during your journey with motherhood.

As you explore all of the different methods that go into mothering, you will find the ones that work best for you. To be a mother does not mean that you know the 'correct' answers or steps that you need to follow. This book is meant to teach you how to find your own answers, the ones that work best for you and for your child. You are going to have the confidence that you need to be the best mother you can be. Once you start believing in yourself, you will see that your purpose extends beyond caring for your child. It is about the bond that you create and the future that you two have together.

My name is Yesenia and I am a mother. I am here to help you because I know how it feels to be in your position. Before I gave birth to my daughter, I was a mess. I just wanted what was best for it, and the thoughts consumed my mind on a daily basis. I worried that she wouldn't bond with me, that I wouldn't be enough for her. After 12 hours of labor, she finally made her way into this world. My Avalon was born. Once the doctors put her on my chest, she stopped crying and looked right into my eyes. I just knew that everything would be okay.

I stayed up for hours on end each night after she came home from the hospital. There were some nights that I just felt like I was doing everything long. Each time she was fussy or wouldn't latch during feedings, I questioned my abilities. I couldn't give up, though. She was relying on me. Through my persistence, I was able to surpass any learning curve that I encountered. Believe me, there will be many!

Through my experience, I raised a beautiful young woman who now takes care of me. Her wisdom and kindness make me feel in awe on a daily basis. I want to help you with motherhood, with feeling like you have what it takes. You are so strong and your child is going to admire you from the very first time you have the honor of meeting. Enjoy it as much as you can because it is a fast experience. Before you know it, your little one will be not so little anymore.

Chapter 1:

Giving Birth and Beyond:

Preparing to Meet Your

Child for the First Time

You are getting closer and closer each day. When you think about giving birth to your little one, you might become flooded with excitement and nerves at the same time—both are valid to feel! This is something that you have never experienced before, so it will be sure to stir up some mixed emotions. You are going to do great. As you learn more about the birthing process, you will feel that you have everything that you need to know in order to deliver your baby successfully. This is a big moment, but it is not the only one. It is simply the start of your journey with parenting. Giving birth to your baby is going to be a moment that you never forget. When you can enjoy the experience without having any fears or worries, this is how you are going to keep a great memory. Ask as many questions as you can and find their answers; you need to prepare yourself until you feel secure before the big day arrives.

In my first trimester, I was set on the birth plan that I envisioned. I thought I had it all figured out, but I honestly rushed to create a plan that looked good on paper. It wasn't necessarily the right plan for me. By the time my third trimester rolled around, I panicked—I knew that my at-home water birth was not going to be the right choice. While I wanted things to be calm and as natural as possible, it just wasn't a realistic plan for me at that time. I did what every good mother must learn how to do—I adapted. After reconfiguring my entire birth plan, I was happy with the choices that I made and I felt secure. This gave me the confidence to enjoy my last few moments as a pregnant woman.

The Importance of Having a Birth Plan

When you discuss your birth plan before you are in labor, this gives your OB-GYN the chance to learn what your preferences are. You aren't going to be able to make these decisions while you are in active labor, focusing on birthing your child. This is why the plan should be made ahead of time. There is no deadline for when this plan must be created, but it is a good idea to think about it as early as the first trimester. Consider what you would like your birthing experience to entail.

This is an entirely personalized process that needs no justification. If you have a preference—make sure it is known! This is going to be your birthing experience, not anyone else's. The professionals around you are there to help you and when you give them a plan, they will have a great guideline to follow. While some births do not go according to plan, it is still a good idea to create one for yourself. You will have the peace of mind in knowing what is likely to happen and how certain situations will be dealt with.

You have probably imagined your experience with giving birth. There is a lot of commotion and uncertainty as you wait until your baby is ready to make their grand entrance into the world. There does not have to be chaos in the delivery room. First, the staff is there to make sure that things are on track and that you and the baby are healthy. They are going to be the foundation of your birthing experience. Anyone else you have in the room with you is going to serve as a support system. When you have these comforts present, you will be able to relax into the experience and feel like everything is going to be okay.

The decisions to be made for your birth plan will cover things such as whether you want the epidural or not and if you would like certain music to be playing or lights to be on. These are custom preferences that you will get to decide. When it comes to your birth plan, there is no request that is going to be "too much." You need to prioritize your comfort so you are not stressed out while you give birth. Remember, your aim is to focus on your happiness, even from the very early stages of motherhood. You need to do what feels right and what will make you feel relaxed. By eliminating as many stressors as possible, your birth plan will serve as a way to obtain a little peace of mind.

The following is a template that you can use to create your own standard vaginal birth plan:

Background Details

This section of your birth plan is going to be simple. It will include your name, your baby's due date, your doctor/midwife/doula contact information, the location where you would like to give birth, the name and contact information of your birthing partner (normally, the spouse), and any important medical issues present.

This first part of your birth plan is meant to provide key information that you can use for reference. While most of it is just factual, there are a few things that you must think about as you create this section. Which hospital would you like to give birth in? If you do not want to give birth in a hospital, is there a birthing center that you would prefer? The choice is up to you and it does depend on the doctors that you have already been seeing. It makes sense to stay at the facility that you are already used to.

When it comes to your birthing partner, this is the person that is going to be your right-hand support. They will be there with you from beginning to end. In your birth plan, you can specify who is to be allowed in the delivery room (many people allow more than one person) and who is going to be designated as the main birthing partner. In case you cannot respond during labor, your birthing partner will be the one who is consulted by the doctors. This is why most people pick their significant other for the role.

During Labor

This section of your birthing plan can list the positions that you would like to try as you give birth. There are many different positions with unique benefits. It is recommended that you do some research to figure out which ones you would be most comfortable with. There is also a decision that you might have to make if your labor does not progress—would you like to be induced? In this section, you would either give your consent or not give your consent.

Pain is something that will need to be effectively managed during labor. This is one thing that new mothers worry about the most. List which medications you are comfortable with taking to help with your pain. This is where you would indicate if you would like the epidural or not.

Some other things to include in this section are comfort measures that you prefer that are non-medicinal. These can include receiving massages, moving around the room, and dimming the lights, or playing your favorite relaxing music. You can also request to spend part of your labor in a water tub or on a ball.

Giving Birth

If you end up needing a C-section for whatever reason, you can indicate which anesthesia option you prefer.

While you might want a vaginal delivery, that isn't always going to be possible. Keep an open mind and understand that you should always have a backup plan.

Do you want to opt for an episiotomy? This is a procedure done to help you give birth. By placing a small surgical cut on your vaginal opening, this is going to help you deliver. It is not mandatory by any means, but many mothers choose this option because of the possibility of the perineum tearing during delivery. It is also thought that the episiotomy is going to heal better than a natural tear.

Indicate where you would like your birthing partner to stand. Also, do you want your birthing partner to film or photograph the delivery? These are very personal preferences that the two of you can discuss prior to putting them in the birth plan. It is always a good thing to make sure that you are both on the same page.

After the Delivery

Once you give birth, do you want your baby to be placed directly on your chest? Some mothers opt for the baby to be handed to the birthing partner first.

Would you like the doctors to discuss any potential procedures that take place before they are administered to your newborn?

Do you plan on breastfeeding? If so, would you like the lactation consultant to help you breastfeed for the first time?

Are there any cultural traditions that you would like to observe after you give birth? List them in detail here.

Who would you like to cut the umbilical cord?

Do you have any preferences for your baby's first bath?

Another great thing to indicate is your preference for visitors. Naturally, you are going to have a lot of people interested in meeting your newborn, but you might prefer to spend some time alone to bond at first. Indicate when you want visitors to come and how many people you will allow to visit.

Natural or C-Section: That's the Big Question

There are pros and cons to each option. The easiest way to decide which is right for you will be through a consultation with your doctor. In this meeting, you can express any worries or concerns to your doctor. From there, you will be guided through the process of each one. Of course, you cannot always plan for having a natural birth versus a C-section birth, but you are allowed to have a preference. Don't feel guilty if you choose a C-section over the possibility of vaginal birth. There are many stigmas that surround this choice that can make future mothers feel that they are lesser than if they do not deliver vaginally. This just isn't true—you need to do what is best for you and your baby.

You must carefully weigh your options. While you might strive for a natural birth, you also need to take your current health into consideration. Many times, there can be health issues that stand in the way of you delivering naturally. Again, this will be covered when you consult your doctor. Knowing that you are in good health to deliver your baby naturally is the first step to making this choice a part of your birth plan. As mentioned, you will need to keep an open mind that a C-section delivery might be the better option for you.

When selecting the natural birth option, it is important that you do some research on the different birthing positions that you can try. By having this knowledge ahead of time, you will be prepared to make your delivery as efficient as possible. The following are some of the most popular positions:

- **Hands and Knees**: This position is exactly as it sounds and it takes the pressure off of your spine. This can be a great choice if you are experiencing back pain during labor. It can also help to boost your baby's oxygen level. This position does take a lot of arm strength, so your arms can get tired.
- **Lying on Your Side**: When you are on your side, it can be easier to relax while you are experiencing contractions. This is another position that allows your baby's oxygen to flow

freely. The downside of this one is that it can be more difficult for your doctor to have access to hearing your baby's heartbeat during delivery.

- **Reclining**: By reclining in the bed and putting the soles of your feet together, you will relax the tension in your muscles. This is also a good alternative if you do not feel comfortable lying down completely. Being propped up can work against gravity at times, though.

- **Birthing Bar**: The birthing bar can be added to your labor bed as an additional form of support. You are meant to lean forward onto it. When you use a birthing bar, this expands your pelvis, making delivery easier. Also, gravity is working in your favor. This is something that you definitely need to request in your birth plan to ensure that the hospital has it.

- **Birthing Stool in Water**: If you want to have your baby in a water tub, using a birthing stool can be a nice component. You can squat on the stool or use it to help you stay propped up on your hands and knees, both helpful while in the water. This can help the baby travel further down, increase dilation, and relieve your back pain. One con that comes with this method is potential blood loss, but this is something that you can discuss with your doctor to safely assess the risk.

If you decide that a C-section sounds better for you, you can plan your delivery date. A planned C-section gives you the peace of mind in knowing when your little one is supposed to arrive. You will have plenty of time to pack your hospital bag and to get there. You will have to get induced, but the process should probably go quickly from there. The doctors are going to guide you through the procedure and they will still follow your given birth plan. When you have a C-section, this lowers your baby's risk of birth injuries. Asphyxia occurs when the umbilical cord wraps around the baby's neck. During a C-section, your medical team will be able to prevent this from occurring.

Naturally, you are also going to experience less stress on your pelvic area and less trauma on your vagina. If you want to plan your C-section, you do not have to feel ashamed or not like a "real mother." Know that many women cannot deliver naturally due to several reasons, whether they physically cannot do it or they decide that a C-section is preferable. You have still carried your baby for these nine months and you are going to be a great mother. Do what feels right to you and make sure to discuss all of your options with your doctor. While you don't have to decide within the first trimester, it does help to start giving it some thought right away so you can confirm your birth plan.

Doulas

During your pregnancy, you should consider hiring a doula. This is going to be your right-hand support system throughout your labor and delivery. Typically, you met one another earlier into your pregnancy for additional support and the chance to become familiar with one another. Having a doula present when you deliver is like having a birth coach there to encourage you. Whether you need additional emotional support or reminders of what to do physically, your doula will be there for you. After you give birth, your doula might also meet up with you once or twice to ensure that you have the hang of breastfeeding and getting your baby to latch.

Most mothers feel relief in their anxiety when they have a doula present during delivery. Because of this, you might have to spend less time in labor because you will feel confident enough to deliver your baby thanks to your doula's help. It has been seen that most mothers also experience fewer emergency C-sections when they have a doula present. A doula can also help you create a strong mother-baby bond after you give birth. Doulas are not medical professionals, but they do typically go through a certification course. They are usually mothers and compassionate individuals that want to help make your birthing experience a great one.

Staying Open-Minded

Know that your birth plan can change at any given second. Childbirth is a wonderfully unpredictable experience. While you might be set on a natural birth with no pain medication, this can change and you should know that this is okay. An emergency might come up that puts you or the baby at risk. Some mothers even find that they must have an emergency C-section when they cannot deliver their baby vaginally, and it begins to pose a health risk.

No matter what happens in the delivery room, know that you are a strong and capable woman. You need to do what is best for the baby and that might be something unplanned. Your doctor and medical staff are going to be there for you every step of the way. Know that you can speak up at any point that you feel you need more help or encouragement. This is your birthing experience and you need to be as comfortable as possible during the entire process.

Meeting Your Baby for the First Time

If there are no complications during delivery, you will be handed your baby immediately after you give birth. The only other time when this wouldn't happen is if you give them the go-ahead to hand the baby over to your birthing partner. This is a magical moment between a parent and a child. At this moment at the hospital, everything will fade away and all of your challenges will feel well worth it. You did it! You carried and delivered a baby—that is amazing. Skin-to-skin contact is how you are going to bond with your baby and show them that you are there to care for them. It is something that you should continue, even after you bring your baby home.

Skin-to-skin contact calms your baby down quickly. When they can feel your skin and hear your heartbeat, they are comforted because it reminds them of being back in the familiarity of the womb. It can also calm you down greatly, assuring you that you are doing everything right to keep your baby happy. Because your baby will feel comfortable and at peace, you should notice less crying. It can be difficult as a first-time mom to deal with a very fussy baby. This crying can be heartbreaking, especially when your efforts don't seem to help. Try using skin-to-skin contact for a quick way to diffuse any situation. Your baby will respond well to it.

Aside from it feeling comfortable to both you and the baby, this type of contact releases important hormones. They will keep your baby's temperature within a normal range, keep their breathing stable, calm their heart rate, and keep their blood sugar level. The hormones that are released to help you will make you feel that your stress level has been lowered and that healing has begun. Skin-to-skin contact has even been noted for keeping your baby's immune system strong, which is very important for a newborn. Enjoy this time with your little one as much as possible. This is just the beginning of your wonderful bond.

Expectations

You have probably imagined this moment, directly after delivery, for some time. From predicting how your baby will look to what they will sound like, these expectations in your head are what fill the space of curiosity. Now, you don't have to imagine because they are going to be right there in front of you. Things might be different than you imagined, but this is all a part of the gift of motherhood. Learning how to adapt is one of the ways to become a great parent. You need to be flexible and willing to learn a lot along the way. This learning process never ends, even as your child grows up.

Newborns experience nine stages immediately after they are born, with the first hour being very important. Here is what you can expect:

1. **The Birth Cry**: You've done it—you've successfully delivered your baby! One of the very first realizations that you will have of this moment is when you hear your baby cry for the first time. This happens as your baby's lungs expand after leaving the womb. It is a great big welcome to the world.

2. **Relaxation**: During this stage, you can expect your baby to remain fairly still. Their hands will be relaxed while their mouths remain idle. This comes after the baby has been soothed after their birth cry. Usually, your baby will be skin-to-skin on your chest and covered by a blanket to protect them from too much stimulus.

3. **Awakening**: Once your baby wakes from the relaxation stage, they will exhibit head and shoulder movements. You will normally see this

happening about three minutes after birth. During this time, your baby will probably open their eyes and start to have some mouth movements. This is the first exploration that your baby will have.

4. **Activity**: Your baby is going to make increased movements and even sounds. You might notice some sucking motions that are made with the mouth. This becomes a natural reflex and your baby will display it often. You can expect the activity stage to begin around eight minutes after birth.

5. **Rest**: During the first hour, your baby is going to rest in increments. Any motion or activity will usually make your baby feel very tired since everything is so new. You can expect your baby to rest between any given stages for varied periods of time. This is normal and healthy.

6. **Crawling**: Not as it sounds, your baby won't be crawling around the room just yet. This stage represents your baby making movements toward the breast for feeding. Through short actions, your baby will also likely be able to reach the nipple. You can expect this to happen around 35 minutes after your baby is born.

7. **Familiarization**: Your baby is going to become familiar with you around 45 minutes after they are born. During this process, you will find

them touching the breast and reaching their mouth toward the nipple. This process can last for around 20 minutes as your baby gets used to the idea of breastfeeding.

8. **Suckling**: It is around an hour after birth that your baby will likely feed for the first time. When they reach this stage, this signifies that they are able to attach to the nipple and suckle. If you had anesthesia during labor, it can take a little bit of extra time for your baby to reach this stage.

9. **Sleep**: This stage occurs when your baby enters a restful sleep. Honestly, you might join them! You have both been through a lot. Once the baby has become acquainted with all of the surroundings and experienced feeding, this will promote the sleep stage. This can happen around 1 ½-2 hours after being born.

Know that you are likely going to feel exhausted, so it is okay if you are feeling fatigued during this whole process. Give yourself credit for what you have been through. Your mind and body are going to need to rest before things truly feel that they have fallen into place. It is important to eat and stay hydrated once you feel up to it. After you give birth, you are likely going to feel pretty weak and dehydrated. Make sure that you put in your requests for your favorite foods and beverages to replenish your energy.

If you find that you are not capable of holding your baby or bonding immediately after giving birth, you are not alone. There are many mothers that feel so fatigued that they must enter a period of rest immediately after the delivery. Know that your baby will be well taken care of, whether in the hands of your birthing partner or the hospital nursery. You do not have to punish yourself if you feel that you cannot jump right into skin-to-skin contact and breastfeeding.

After you get adequate rest, everything will fall into place. Your baby isn't going to be upset with you because you need to take this time. You have just spent nine months carrying them in your womb! For that, you already have a reason to be so proud of yourself. Not to mention, you have overcome one of the biggest challenges: childbirth. Do what you can and bond with your baby as much as possible, but also, listen to your body. Take a long period of rest and allow yourself to feel rejuvenated.

Chapter 2:

Breastfeeding and All

Questions Food-Related

Breastfeeding is a topic that you are going to have lots of questions about. This is natural because you have never experienced it before. While there is a lot you can do to prepare for the experience, the process can differ greatly once your baby arrives. There are a lot of factors that surround a successful breastfeeding experience. While you cannot guarantee that your baby is going to know how to latch and feed instantly, you can prepare yourself to help them and make the process easier. In this chapter, you are not only going to learn important breastfeeding tips but also about obstacles that might stand in your way. From your feeding schedule to what you need to do if you cannot breastfeed, you will have all the answers you need.

After I gave birth to my daughter, I imagined I would enter the nine newborn stages according to plan. I could see myself successfully getting her to latch on my own and feeling great accomplishment from this. When she was born, I was met with an entirely different experience. At the time, I felt like a failure because I was unable to feed her. We had our skin-to-skin bonding and she started exhibiting the signs of wanting to eat. Great! I thought that I had it made. When I brought her up to my breast, she just wouldn't latch. Even the hospital staff had trouble helping me with this dilemma. She ended up being bottle-fed for her first meal. This was not how I envisioned it at all. I felt so much pressure to be a good, breastfeeding mom. To think that I couldn't make it happen devastated me. Through time, I learned that this is normal. Not every mother can breastfeed immediately and that is okay. It takes a lot of practice and trial and error.

Before Baby Arrives

You are going to need some supplies before your baby is born. To prepare, use the checklist below:

- Breast Pump
- Breast Pump accessories and cleaning supplies
- Nursing Bras (two regular and two for sleeping)
- Nursing Nightgown
- Nursing Pajamas
- Robe
- 2 Nursing Tanks
- 2 Nursing Tops
- Breast Milk Storage Bags
- Breast Milk Freezing Trays
- Breast Shells (for sore nipples)
- Nipple Shield

- Nipple Cream
- Hydrogel Pads
- Warm/Cool Packs
- Compression Top
- Abdominal Support Band
- 1-2 Packages Disposable Nursing Pads
- 1-2 Packages Washable Nursing Pads
- Hand Sanitizer
- Brush for Cleaning Bottles
- Microwave Steam Sterilizer Bags

You can have all of the necessities, but you still might feel like you need additional support with breastfeeding. If this is the case, you can contact La Leche League. They are an organization that provides support to mothers around the world. Founded in 1956, LLL was founded by a group of mothers just like you. Their aim was to provide support with breastfeeding because they knew first-hand of its challenges. Through the resources that you can find on their website, you will be able to read a lot of valuable information that will help you on your own breastfeeding journey. They also have a feature that allows you to search for local support, in case you are looking for some in-person reassurance.

Getting comfortable with breastfeeding is a combination of knowing how to do it and making your space accessible and practical. Create a haven for yourself where you plan on breastfeeding. To do this, you can make sure that you have all of your supplies nearby, as well as the proper garments and nursing pads. Your baby is going to eat every few hours, so it is important that you have all of this stuff set up ahead of time. This is going to be especially handy for those middle-of-the-night feedings. When you feel that you have everything you need within reach, you can focus on your baby and make sure that they are being nourished. It takes away a lot of stress and pressure, too.

It does not matter where you decide to breastfeed, whether it is in your baby's nursery or in your own bedroom. It is wise to set up a haven for yourself in both rooms because you never know when and where your baby will need to eat. In the nursery, you can make sure that there is a comfortable chair available for you to use. A rocking chair works great because this can simultaneously soothe the baby into sleep. Getting into a great routine will also get you confident and comfortable with breastfeeding. If you feed your baby at the same time each day, this will get them acclimated to their feedings. They might respond in a less fussy way when they know that food is coming soon. This also allows you to have a somewhat manageable schedule that will allow you to get some sleep!

Don't forget to involve your significant other! Though they won't be breastfeeding, it is absolutely possible for them to be a part of the process. Your partner can meet with a lactation consultant with you. When they understand the methods that should be used and the tips that are given, they can help you implement them. Your partner can also help by doing small chores such as making sure that you have clean nursing pads and making sure that there are clean bottles for you to use if you pump. Most mothers believe that they are in this alone, but they don't have to be. If you choose, you can involve your partner as much as you'd like. This creates an even stronger bond that is based on your newborn.

After Baby Arrives

Once your baby is born, you will probably breastfeed within the first few hours of birth. If this does not happen, remember that everybody is different. Your body is only capable of so much, and it deserves to rest after all of the work that it has done. The time that you spend at the hospital with your baby will be one of learning. There will be staff there to guide you if you have any questions or concerns about breastfeeding. For most mothers, latching is the most difficult part. When your baby doesn't want to latch, this can feel very disappointing. Know that your baby is going through this for the first time, too. You both have to get used to the process. If your baby doesn't latch, this doesn't make you a failure. Like anything else that you are great at, practice is required.

Going home from the hospital is a very big step. It is your chance to finally be in your home environment with your little one. With the exception of a couple of doula visits (if you have a doula), you and your significant other are going to be alone to make choices for the care of your baby. There will be no medical professional present to advise you and no team dedicated to your progress. It is a huge step for new parents, one that should be taken with confidence and pride. You brought your baby into this world! For that, you can give yourself credit already. Now, you must rely on your motherly instincts to care for your little one.

Getting a Good Latch

The secret to getting your baby to latch depends on the positioning. Your position, as well as the baby's position, should be taken into account. One way to help you is to line your baby up with yourself, belly-to-belly. This means that your baby's nose should line up with your nipple. When you get into this position, your baby will not have to turn their head to latch. It makes the process a lot easier and a lot more likely to happen on the first few tries. This should provide you with a deep latch that only requires your baby to open their mouth and tilt their head back slightly. It also happens to be a comfortable position for you, as well.

Another tip is to slow down the process of latching. Many mothers want to put their baby right up to the nipple and expect them to start eating right away. The baby needs to become accustomed to breastfeeding, even after it has already happened a few times. Try to wait for your baby to open their mouth before you bring them close to your breast. This process will happen on its own without you having to coax your baby into it. If they are hungry, they will naturally show you this by opening their mouth. Even when you feel impatient or worried that your baby is not going to eat, believe that their natural instincts will kick in.

Avoid holding the back of your baby's head in place in an effort to position them to latch. This creates a rigid structure and might make them less likely to latch. The reflex of reaching for the nipple and opening their mouth should happen naturally. When you allow this to happen naturally, you are giving your baby the chance to develop their reflexes, which is important. Again, as much as you might want to try to help, the best thing that you can do is to position your baby belly-to-belly and keep their nose in line with your nipple. The rest will happen naturally in time. There are no deeper secrets to getting your baby to latch. Consider that your baby is not always going to be in the mood to breastfeed, so don't worry if it doesn't happen like clockwork. They will let you know when they are ready to eat.

Once your baby latches successfully, you do not need to set a timer or count the minutes. They are going to eat until they feel full. This might be for two minutes or this might be for 10 minutes. Your baby might want to take only one breast, or they might want to divide their time between both. Once they finish up feeding on the first breast, you can offer the second one to make sure that they are finished. There are no particular benefits to your baby feeding from one breast or both. It all comes down to your baby's preference and mood during the breastfeeding session.

As your baby is learning how to breastfeed, know that it is recommended to avoid pacifiers at first. The AAP (American Academy of Pediatrics) suggests that giving your baby a pacifier too early can result in missed hunger cues. Your baby will suck on the pacifier instead of latching on to breastfeed, thinking that this will provide the same source of nourishment. Once your baby has successfully mastered the art of latching, you can introduce the pacifier if you wish. This will give them time to learn how to breastfeed without any confusion.

If sitting upright is not working for your baby or for your own comfort, you can try lying down on your side. This still allows you to place the baby in the optimal position without having to hold as much of their weight. It can be a comfortable position if you are feeding late at night or early in the morning because you can breastfeed in your bed. This also serves as a great position for mothers who had C-sections, taking pressure off of the stomach as you hold your baby. A nursing stool is also another valid option if you feel like you need more support while trying to get your baby to latch. Nursing stools give you more lap space and relieve pressure from your body. This becomes especially helpful if you went through an episiotomy or if you are shorter in stature.

Dealing with Discomfort

Breastfeeding can become a challenging task because it can get rather uncomfortable. There are not too many ways around this, but you should feel proud of yourself because you are feeding your baby and keeping them healthy. There are some tricks that you can use to combat soreness, leakage, and cracked skin. When you can maintain a healthy level of self-care as you breastfeed, these symptoms should not be too difficult for you to handle. It all becomes a process of being able to listen to your body and know the difference between discomfort and pain.

When your baby latches on, this might feel weird at first. Know that you will get used to the feeling. Breastfeeding might be foreign to you, but you will soon get used to all that comes along with it. If you ever experience sharp pain, this could be a sign that you need to contact your doctor or a lactation consultant. The pain from breastfeeding should be more of a discomfort rather than something that debilitates you. Listen to your body and you will know if the pain is too intense. Getting these issues addressed sooner rather than later will help you successfully breastfeed in the future. There is no need to feel embarrassed or ashamed—many other mothers experience it, too!

Your nipples go through a lot during breastfeeding. If you need some relief, use hydrogel pads. This will help them from getting too dry and cracked. The pads supply your nipples with necessary moisture in between feedings, plus they are safe for your baby to breastfeed after using them. If your nipples become sore, the best thing you can do is take any pressure off of them. This includes wearing loose-fitting clothing and bras that are not too constricting. When you do this, it will allow you to keep breastfeeding your baby. Make sure that you are aware that products such as fragrances, laundry detergent, and deodorant can irritate your nipples further. Make sure that you only use gentle fragrances, or that you refrain from using them at all.

You can try to change breastfeeding positions if you find that your usual one is too hard on your nipples. This is all going to depend on what feels best to you and what your baby responds well to. Don't be afraid to try a lot of different nursing positions until you find the one that works best for both of you. Your breasts are going to be tender and a lot heavier during this time. You have likely experienced this type of pain through past PMS that you've had. If you need some relief, you can take some Ibuprofen to ease the inflammation.

Since your breasts are producing a lot of milk, it is common to experience leakage. If this happens, you can wear pads in your nursing bra to soak up any leakage that happens. You can also try breastfeeding your baby more often. Even if your sessions are short, breastfeeding more often will lead to some more room in your breasts and will prevent leakage from happening. If your baby cannot drink the milk as quickly as it is being produced, you can pump more often. This will provide you with relief while also giving you the chance to stock up on breastmilk that will be easy to access in the future.

In rare cases, milk backup can lead to a condition known as mastitis. Approximately every one in 10 mothers experience it while breastfeeding. Your milk might be backed up because you are producing an abundance with little relief, or because your baby is not latching properly. This causes an infection that becomes painful and will prevent you from being able to breastfeed. If you start to experience flu-like symptoms, you should consult your doctor right away. You should also notice heat and inflammation coming from the breast that is experiencing mastitis. Other symptoms include discharge coming from your nipple and lumps forming in your breast. This can happen because your milk duct is clogged and it causes your breast to swell.

How to Make Breastfeeding Enjoyable

As the mother, you need to make sure that you are taking care of yourself to take care of your baby. Dehydration is commonly experienced by new mothers who are breastfeeding. It becomes easy to forget to drink water because you are so focused on getting your baby to drink breast milk. If you need to, set reminders for yourself to stay hydrated. Water is always the best thing that you can drink to rehydrate yourself. Sugary drinks, such as juice or soda, will only leave you feeling thirsty. Think about the water you drink as more fuel for your body to keep producing healthy breast milk.

Wait until your baby knows how to successfully latch before you introduce a pacifier into the routine. As mentioned, your baby might have confusion or delays present when you give them a pacifier. Instead of latching onto your breast, they will learn how to suck on the pacifier, but that will not nourish them. While you are going through an incredible learning experience, so is your little one. You need to give them a chance to adapt to the routine that you set in place.

You have probably worried about running out of breast milk and having to feed your baby formula to supplement for the loss. Don't worry too much about this. Your body will naturally produce more milk the more that you breastfeed. Each time that you feed your baby, you are sending signals to your body saying that it should keep producing breast milk. The supply will steadily increase for the duration of your time breastfeeding. This is also how your body knows how to stop producing milk once your baby is old enough to eat solid foods.

Consider that your diet is going to directly impact your baby's diet. While they are not receiving nutrients from you directly through the womb any longer, they are still being fed fractions of what you eat through your breast milk. Consider adding the following foods to your diet to encourage a healthy supply of breast milk:

- Fish and Seafood: salmon, shellfish, seaweed, and sardines
- Meat: beef, pork, lamb, and organ meats
- Fruits and Vegetables: berries, cabbage, tomatoes, kale, garlic, and broccoli
- Nuts and seeds: walnuts, chia seeds, almonds, flaxseeds, and hemp seeds
- Other Foods: eggs, potatoes, quinoa, oats, buckwheat, and dark chocolate

All of the above foods are going to nourish you. Try to stick with natural foods and all-natural ingredients when you cook. Eating too much artificially processed food is what limits the nourishment that you receive. In turn, your baby will also be receiving less nourishment.

Be aware that you cannot take certain medications while breastfeeding. Most OTC (over-the-counter) medication is safe. It has been said that pain relievers such as Tylenol and Advil are both okay to take while you are breastfeeding. They contain acetaminophen and ibuprofen, so you can also take the generic brands of each. If you are ever unsure if something is going to be unsafe for your baby, you can always consult your doctor first. Avoid anything that offers "extra strength" properties because this might be too intense. Also, make sure that you are taking the smallest dose possible because the medicine does travel through your bloodstream and directly into your milk ducts.

Remember that breastfeeding is natural, and you should not feel ashamed if you have to do it in public. If you are comfortable breastfeeding without a covering, don't feel pressured into using one. However, use one if that is what you want to do. Part of being a breastfeeding first-time mother comes with identifying how confident you feel. If you have the confidence, use it and enjoy the experience. It does not last forever. This is one of the most intimate bonding experiences that you will have with your little one. If you do encounter negativity for breastfeeding, know that you are your baby's parent. It is up to you to care for them and to keep them safe. Trust in your ability to make the best decisions for your baby. As a first time mom, many people will give you their opinions, both unsolicited and warranted. You don't always have to listen. As long as your baby is safe and happy, you are doing a wonderful job.

What to Do if Breastfeeding Isn't an Option

There are certain factors that will make breastfeeding impossible. Lactation failure is not very common, but it can happen. This occurs when your body simply does not make enough milk. You might stay hydrated and your baby knows how to latch, but the breast milk just does not get produced. There are many reasons for lactation failure. Some mothers experience this due to hormonal complications, while others experience it from having thyroid abnormalities. Your doctor should be able to shed some light on your own unique situation if you find yourself experiencing lactation failure.

In some cases, your body produces breast milk, yet it is not safe for you to breastfeed. If you have a chronic illness that requires prescription medication, this can become a safety hazard for your baby. Of course, this is not your fault because you did not choose your illnesses. If you find yourself in this position, you might feel very guilty for not being able to breastfeed. Learn how to let go of this guilt by understanding that there are still plenty of ways for you to feed your baby. This does not mean that you are a bad mother or a failure.

It is common for some babies to never learn how to latch on, despite your attempts. This is especially common for premature babies. No matter how many positions or techniques you try, your baby might never get the hang of latching on. For a situation like this, you should still be able to pump your breast milk and feed your baby from a bottle. There are always ways that you can work around these challenges. There are also instances where your baby might have a physical disability that makes it hard for them to latch. An example of this is when a baby is born with a cleft lip or palate. Being a mother automatically encourages you to use your creativity and problem-solving skills.

If you are in a position to pump your breast milk, but cannot breastfeed, an electric pump will make things easier for you. Since you are going to be pumping frequently, using a device that works automatically will probably fit in well with your schedule. If you do have to use formula to feed your baby, know that it is still full of plenty of nutrients. A lot of mothers tend to look down on feeding formula to newborns, but each situation is different. You should not be made to feel guilty for bottle feeding. There are many different types of formula to choose from, so you can regain some control over your baby's nutrition by doing some research and selecting the most beneficial brand.

You have probably heard that breastfed babies are healthier and smarter than bottle-fed babies. Some studies have been done in recent years that refute these theories, though. According to one study done on health, there were no distinct differences in the number of common colds caught by babies. Therefore, it suggests that breastfeeding does not boost the immune system as much as it was once thought. For illnesses that include diarrhea, nine percent of breastfed babies contracted them while thirteen percent of formula-fed babies contracted them. This difference is not very substantial when you compare the statistics. For skin conditions such as eczema, three percent of breastfed babies had it while six percent of bottle-fed babies had it. This difference is also not very staggering when you compare the two.

In the end, the choice is yours to either breastfeed or not breastfeed. If you are able to, this does not automatically mean that you have to. Motherhood is founded on many choices that you will have to make throughout the years. Just because something is considered normal and socially accepted does not mean that this is the same route you have to take. Give yourself a chance to fully explore your options, and make the best decisions from there. Some people might not agree with your choices, but this matters less than what is truly best for your baby. You will learn how to bypass the naysayers and feel confident in the decisions that you are making. This is how you will become the best mom possible, overlooking the judgment and focusing on caring for your baby.

Chapter 3:

Baby Soothing and

Sleeping Arrangements

You know what they say—once your baby is born, say goodbye to your sleep schedule. This can be a difficult transition for a lot of new moms, but it doesn't have to be all bad. When you know how to soothe your baby and make their sleep space as comfortable as possible, you will create a routine that will allow both of you to get enough rest. This chapter will break down all that you can do for your baby, whether they are feeling fussy or restless. By working with your partner, the two of you will come together to create a schedule that allows you to take turns soothing the crying baby. This is a great way to maximize your energy and to prevent both of you from getting burnt out at the same time.

Being a mom takes some detective work. Since your baby cannot communicate yet, you must figure out what is wrong and then come up with solutions to soothe them. Once you are able to get a few hours of quality sleep again, you will feel so thankful that you tried these tips to get your baby to sleep through the night. All babies are different, but these methods are designed to soothe even the fussiest newborns. If something doesn't work at first, give it some time. Babies operate well on schedules, and it takes time to create a schedule that works for you and for your family.

Soothing a Crying Baby

There is nothing worse than the sound of your baby crying, no matter why they are crying. When you hear this sound, take a few seconds to observe why they are upset. There are many different cries that you will begin to recognize—a hunger cry, a tired cry. Because there are minimal ways for your baby to communicate, your baby is going to learn that crying will get your attention quickly. Since you always tend to them when they cry, this teaches them that they are going to get a response from you. Don't forget to check their diaper because having a dirty diaper can also become a reason that your baby is feeling upset. There also might be discomfort due to the baby's clothing or the way that the clothing fits. Make sure that it isn't too tight or rubbing against their skin harshly.

If you cannot identify why your baby won't stop crying, they might be experiencing colic. This is a condition that causes intense and prolonged crying that can be very worrisome to a new mother. Because there is no apparent reason for colic, you will find that your baby does not respond to any of the comforting techniques that you try. If you feel that your baby seems to fit the symptoms, you can consult your doctor for an official diagnosis. The good thing is that colic will go away on its own. It usually stops when your baby reaches around four months in age. In some cases, it will stop even sooner than that. Colic is common for newborns and it should not cause you any alarm. Remember to be patient if you find that your baby has it and know that you are doing your best.

When you have covered the bases of making sure that your baby is clean, warm, and well-fed, you can try the following techniques to get them to stop crying:

- **Swaddling**: When you swaddle your baby in a blanket, this helps them to feel more secure. The tightness of the blanket offers them protection and comfort. Many experts believe that babies stop crying once they are swaddled because this reminds them of what it is like to be inside of the womb. Typically, your baby's arm should be inside of the blanket, but some babies enjoy it more when their arms are left outside. You will have to try different types of swaddling to see which ones your baby responds to.

- **Calming Sounds/Music**: Babies are very responsive to rhythmic noises. Whether you put on a calming soundtrack or make the noises yourself, try to give your baby a soothing environment that will promote relaxation. If you cannot access music and you need to soothe your baby, you can try rhythmic shushing noises. Hearing the "shhh, shhh, shhh," will often be enough to grasp your baby's attention, encouraging them to focus on the sound instead of crying. A white noise machine might also be a good investment for your nursery.

- **Body Carrier**: When you wear a body carrier, your baby gets the chance to be close to you. Hearing your heartbeat and feeling your skin might be enough to calm your baby down. This also provides you with a great way to care for your baby while keeping your hands free to do other things. As a new mom, you will realize that multitasking becomes a part of your daily routine. If your baby does not respond well to the carrier at first, you might need to give them some time to get used to it. Practice carrying your baby in the carrier every day.

- **Breastfeeding**: When you breastfeed your baby, you aren't only providing nourishment. You are also providing skin-to-skin contact. This is very soothing to a newborn because they feel secure when they can touch your skin. Even if you don't think your baby is very hungry, breastfeeding can be a great way to soothe a crying baby. They might only latch and eat a little bit, but the contact will comfort them enough to cause them to fall asleep.

- **Talking/Singing**: Your baby is used to your voice. Even in the womb, your baby heard you speaking. By talking to your baby in a calming voice or singing to them, this can be enough to remind them that they are safe. Your voice is a built-in comfort to your little one, and you should try to use it whenever possible. No matter what you decide to say or sing, your baby is not going to judge you. As long as they can hear you, this will be enough of a reminder that they are not alone.

- **Massage**: You know how great a massage feels, and your baby will likely agree. Start by massaging their chest while they are on their back. Use small, circular motions to go from the center outward. You can also make small circles on their stomach. Rolling their arms and legs gently between your palms can also be enough to soothe them. As you massage your baby, you can also talk or sing. This can become a nice ritual for both of you, providing a nice way for you to bond.

- **The Colic Carry**: Even if your baby does not have colic, this carry can prove to be helpful. Start by laying your baby on their stomach over your forearm, their head to the side and resting in your open palm. You can take your other hand to rub their back and stabilize them. An alternative position is to lay your baby across your lap. You can use your needs to provide stabilization. Much like any other soothing method, you can try out different positions to see which ones your baby responds best to.

- **Help From Your Partner**: Don't forget that you can enlist your partner for help! They can try almost all of these soothing methods, too. As a mom, there will be plenty of times where you feel that you've reached your limit—this is normal. No matter how much you love your little one, the stress that comes with parenting does not discriminate. Even long-time moms can feel it. You can make a schedule with your partner to take turns soothing the baby when they start crying. This will prevent both of you from getting burnt out.

- **What *Not* to Do**: Never shake your crying baby. This can result in shaken baby syndrome, an often fatal syndrome that comes from being too rough while trying to console them. In as little as five seconds of shaking, this can result in brain damage to your fragile baby. It can be a natural instinct to shake your baby when they are inconsolable, even if you never intend on hurting them. No matter what the situation is, this will always make them more upset, or it will harm them. Because their brain is not fully developed yet, it is easy for the shaking motion to cause the brain to rattle inside of the skull. While you might never even consider harming your child, it is important to know how easily that this can happen, even if you don't intend on shaking them hard.

Sleeping Arrangements

Not all babies are going to immediately take to their cribs. While you might have the most beautiful nursery set up in anticipation of your baby's arrival, know that you will likely have to experiment with various sleeping arrangements until your baby is able to sleep through the night. These are some arrangements that you can try. What works one night might not work every single night, so try not to get discouraged. Your baby will learn how to sleep through the night as they get older, but it does take some patience and different techniques.

Co-Sleeping

Bringing your baby into your bed at night is a decision that you must make with your partner. You need to make sure that it works for your lifestyle and that everyone is going to be able to handle the sleeping arrangement. Co-sleeping has its pros and cons, and it isn't for everyone. If you decide that you do not want to try co-sleeping, this does not make you a bad mother. This is just another decision that you must make as you navigate your parenting journey.

Pros:

- **Comfort**: Your baby is naturally going to feel comfortable when you co-sleep. They get to be between the two people they know best in the world so far. A lot of parents report that there is less crying at night, meaning that everyone gets more sleep. This can be great if your baby tends to wake up frequently. Co-sleeping tends to reduce your baby's separation anxiety, which usually happens when you have a separate nursery. If you do not feel comfortable with your baby in your bed, you can bring their crib into your bedroom, beside your bed. This way, your baby will still be able to see and hear you.

- **Safety**: Since your baby will be able to lay their eyes on you if they wake up in the night, they will feel safe knowing that you are there. Babies do not have a great concept of object permanence. This is why the crying can begin as soon as you leave the room. In their mind, they think that you are gone and they do not know when/if you are coming back. While you might be able to keep an eye on your baby and listen through a baby monitor, your baby is not going to have the same reassurance until their sense of object permanence develops some more.

- **Breastfeeding**: When your baby needs to breastfeed, co-sleeping offers the convenience of already being in the same room. After waking up several times throughout the night, this can leave you disoriented and groggy. Make sure that you have a comfortable seating arrangement so that you can nurse your baby quickly. The sooner that you get them fed, the sooner they will be able to fall back asleep. It can be tempting to just stay seated in your bed, but be aware that falling asleep while you are breastfeeding can be dangerous. This is why having a nursing chair in the room is recommended.

- **Recovery**: No matter what kind of delivery you had, you are still going to need some time to physically heal. When you co-sleep, this allows you to keep your movements down to a minimum. Getting out of bed and going into the baby's nursery each night can be exhausting after you have just given birth. Even in the weeks to follow, your body will still need some time to recuperate. A lot of mothers like to co-sleep in the beginning for this reason.

- **Bonding**: While you might be able to stay at home with your baby temporarily after they are born, your maternity leave is going to come to an end. When you don't get to see your baby much during the day because they are being watched by someone else, they are likely going to be asleep early in the evening. This gives you a small window of time to be together. Co-sleeping offers you an additional chance to bond and to spend time with one another.

- **Trust**: Co-sleeping means that you will be spending several hours in the same room as your baby. This can bring security to both of you. Whether they are asleep or not, you will both be aware of one another's presence. This can build up a great sense of trust and a feeling of security that would not be possible if your baby slept in the nursery. Many people believe that co-sleeping deepens your baby's sense of love that they have for you.

Cons:

- **SIDS**: SIDS (Sudden Infant Death Syndrome) is a devastating and unexplained death that happens to newborns. According to the National Centre for the Review of Prevention of Child Deaths in America, 8,000 of the unexplained infant deaths occurred during co-sleeping. This is not to say that co-sleeping is directly related to SIDS, but it has been seen to increase the risk of it happening.

- **Threads**: Something important to look out for is your baby's risk of being confined by a "toe tourniquet." This means that a loose thread or hair wraps around your baby's toe, causing a loss of circulation. This can happen to their fingers, too. Because your bedsheets are likely not infant-safe, you are taking a risk by bringing your baby into your bed. An easy fix would be to change your bedding during times when you know you will be co-sleeping. Babies love to grab a hold of anything loose that they can get their hands on. Even when you try to prevent this from happening, they might still be able to get a hold of loose threads that you do not notice.

- **Disruption**: As a couple, bedtime is normally quality time that you get to spend with one another. By bringing your baby into your shared bed at night, this cuts down on the amount of alone time that you get together. While mothering is a very important task, so is keeping your relationship with your partner healthy. Co-sleeping can be the cause of marital problems because it can lead to frustration. If you decide to co-sleep, make sure that your partner is also open to the idea, or else there will be a chance for some resentment to form, no matter how much they adore your baby. Another reason that co-sleeping can cause disruption is that it can take away opportunities to engage in sex with your partner. As new parents, you probably expected this, but eliminating this time together can lead to problems within your relationship.

- **Patterns**: The moment you first bring your baby home, you are creating sleep patterns. It is thought that the longer you let your child co-sleep, the harder it will be to get them to sleep on their own in the future. Your baby will possibly become so used to sleeping with you that they will not feel secure enough to be on their own. According to The Norwegian Institute of Public Health, 56,000 mothers were surveyed on their babies' co-sleeping habits. One third of babies that were waking up frequently through the night at six months old were still waking up frequently at 18 months old. It is thought that the prolonged co-sleeping arrangement held them back from developing a sense of independence.

- **Falling**: Your bed is a lot less secure than a crib. There is the risk that your baby will get too close to the edge and fall off of the bed.

Naturally, this is probably a thought that has already crossed your mind while you considered whether or not you were going to co-sleep. There is also the possibility that your baby can become wedged in gaps, such as the gap between your bed and the wall. Even when you place pillows around your baby to protect them while you sleep, there is a risk that they might be able to move beyond them.

- **Overheating**: When your baby is in your bed, there are many blankets around them that they would not normally have if they were in their crib. While you can do your best to keep them uncovered at night, there is still a risk they will become covered up and get overheated. Not to mention, having your body heat and your partner's body heat on either side of your baby can cause them to heat up even more.

Teaching Your Baby to Sleep on Their Own

The alternative route to co-sleeping is to teach your baby how to self-soothe in order to sleep through the night. While it might be difficult, it isn't impossible. You can use these techniques to help make the transition as smooth as possible:

- **Placing Your Baby in the Crib When They Are Dozing**: When you notice that your baby is starting to doze off, whether they are in your bed or in your arms, place them into their crib. This transition does not always work the first time, but it becomes a good opportunity to encourage your newborn to sleep on their own. They will begin to see their crib as a place of comfort each time that they wake up.

- **Remain Present in the Room**: Stay in your baby's nursery until they fall asleep all the way. Sometimes, just having your presence nearby can be enough to relax your baby and convince them to fall asleep. You can sit in your nursing chair so that your baby can see you, but they will not be able to touch you. At first, your baby might cry in protest when they realize that you aren't taking them out of the crib, but they will get used to it over time.

- **Practice Giving Massages Without Holding Them**: You can try to massage your baby, as mentioned above. Without picking them up out of their crib, go through all of the motions of the massages that were listed. This is going to give them a familiar soothing effect while still encouraging them that it is safe to fall asleep in their crib.

- **Understand Why They Are Crying**: As mentioned, you are going to learn exactly what your baby's different cries mean. When your baby starts crying, this does not always mean that they need you to take action and do something for them. To promote self-soothing, do not automatically pick your baby up as soon as they start getting fussy. You can calm them down by talking to them or singing to them, but you can try to do so without automatically picking them up. This is going to teach them that everything will still be okay and that they will get through the feeling.

The Importance of Having a Sleeping Routine

Any routine takes some time to get used to. You cannot expect your sleeping routine to work flawlessly in the very beginning. Both you and your baby are going to have to learn how to accomplish it together. It is going to take patience from you, so be prepared for some exhausting nights. They will prove to be worth it when you have a newborn who can sleep through the night, though. Not only will your sleeping routine help your little one while they are an infant, but it should get them on the right track for when they grow older.

1. **Practice Your Routine**: Once you get set with a routine, you have to commit to it. You are going to bring the regularity into your baby's

life. If you can follow the routine yourself, you are going to set an example for what your baby needs to do. Your baby is naturally going to follow your lead. While it can be tempting to deviate from the routine because it feels easier, know that this is only going to hurt the progress that you have already made. Any routine requires consistency.

2. **Create a Bedtime**: It is never too early to establish a bedtime for your baby. When you can put them to sleep at the same time each night, this is going to help with consistency. Your baby is going to know what to expect the more that you practice this. When you lay your baby down to rest, there should be no need to take them out of their crib again until they need to be changed or fed.

3. **Make a Ritual**: Participate in a soothing ritual with your baby that will signify that sleep is coming soon. Whether you decide to give them a bath or feed them in a dimly lit room, your goal should be relaxation an hour before you put them down for the night. If they are in a noisy or bright environment with a lot of stimulation, sleep is going to be unlikely to follow. They will remain asleep for a longer period of time when they feel relaxed.

4. **Set Night Shifts**: This part involves collaborating with your partner. Before the two of you fall asleep, agree on who is going to get up first if your baby starts crying. Make sure that there are plenty of bottles on hand in case your partner needs to do some late-night feeding. This will allow at least one of you to get some rest while the other tends to the baby. The next time your baby cries, you can switch places. Depending on your individual schedules, you can work out a night shift that is going to serve you best.

5. **Take Advantage of Naps**: If you try to keep your baby awake for the majority of the day, this does not necessarily mean that they are going to sleep through the night. Babies need a lot of periodic rest during daylight hours, so it is okay if they take plenty of naps. You can also use this time to take a nap yourself if you are feeling tired. It is always best to just do what your baby's body wants to do naturally. Trying to purposely keep them awake is only going to disrupt their natural body clock.

6. **Give it Time**: If you encounter a rough night every so often, this is normal. As a new mom, you can expect plenty of them—it is what comes with the territory. Your baby is experiencing many things that are also brand

new to them. You will need to give them time to get used to the sleeping schedule before they get used to it. Some babies work really well on schedules, picking them up immediately. This just depends on how your baby individually responds. No matter what, don't give up. Believe in your sleeping schedule and know that it is going to be beneficial for your baby in the long run.

While your baby is a newborn, there is going to be a lot of trial and error. No new mother knows exactly what must be done, and even the most experienced moms still struggle. Your baby is a wonderful and unique individual. What works for other babies won't always work for yours, so try your best not to compare any situations. If you have other mothers in your life who want to offer you advice, thank them for it and know that you do not always have to take it. Your job as a mother is to use your maternal instincts. Listen to what you believe is right and know that you do know your baby best. The more that you work with your sleeping schedule, the more you will see the results paying off. When you are feeling like you are too exhausted to move, know that this time does not last forever. It will be over before you know it, so enjoy this time that you get to spend with your newborn.

Chapter 4:

Daily Living with a Child

Once you bring your baby home from the hospital, your daily way of life is going to change. While you might return to work at your same job and spend time together as a couple, you now have a wonderful new addition to include in your life. Living with a child changes a lot about the typical routine shared by two adults. There are plenty of new tasks for you to learn in order to make your baby feel comfortable and safe. Most of these things are probably what you have already thought about, but now you are going to learn how to execute them effectively. Like anything that relates to mothering, you are going to become better at it as you practice it. By tuning into your maternal instincts, you will be able to create a beautiful life for your child.

Bathing and Personal Hygiene

When bathing a newborn, remember that this is something that only needs to happen once or twice a week, and only if the umbilical cord has fallen off. If your baby still has their cord, you will have to give them sponge baths. This is because frequent bathing can dry out their fragile skin. As your baby gets older, you can increase this frequency. Bathing your baby can be a very nerve-wracking experience, but you are going to be great at it. No matter what, you should never walk away from your baby while they are bathing. They need constant supervision, even while they are in their infant tub. To get started, make sure that you have an infant bathtub (it will go in the sink or in your regular bathtub), mild soap that does not contain irritants, a soft washcloth, two bath towels, a change of diaper and clothing, and a baby hairbrush.

Once your little one is in the tub, you can follow these simple steps:

- Wash their face with plain water
- Clean their eyes by wiping away any debris in the corners
- Clean the surfaces of their nose and ears (avoiding internal contact with water)
- Wash their body with mild soap
- Rinse them with plain water
- Pat your baby dry with a clean towel
- Take the baby into your arms and massage the shampoo into their head
- Rinse their head thoroughly to avoid any scalp build-up
- Towel dry their hair and then brush it with a soft baby brush

- Dress your baby in a diaper and appropriate clothing

Nail Care

Keep your baby's fingernails trimmer to prevent them from scratching themselves. If there are any rough edges, use a baby nail file to smooth them out. To trip your baby's fingernails safely, hold the skin away from the nail and cut straight across with a pair of baby nail clippers. If you know you need to trim their nails, do so after a bath because the nails will be softer and easier to trim. Another suggestion is to trim their nails while they are sleeping. Your baby might get fussy if they are away while you try to trim them.

Your baby's nails will grow fast, but you do not have to trim them too often. You should make sure that the nails are long enough to cut safely without accidentally cutting any of their surrounding skin. If you need to supplement, you can put mittens over your baby's hands to prevent them from scratching themselves. This is especially helpful while they sleep, as they will not have any control over how they might move their hands.

Ear Care

There is not too much that you will have to do for your baby's ears. In the bath, you are already going to be cleaning the surfaces of their ears, and this is a perfectly adequate way to clean them. You do not want to stick any cotton swabs or other cleaning devices inside of their ear canals because this could rupture your baby's eardrums. Their ears are very fragile, and they can easily be injured. The same can be said about cotton balls— don't use them on your baby's ears, even the surfaces. Residue from these cotton balls can become lodged inside your baby's ears.

If you notice that your baby is constantly trying to touch their ears and crying, this could be an indication that they have an ear infection. Babies commonly develop ear infections, so this is no need for too much concern. As soon as you notice your baby displaying this behavior, you can take them to the doctor and an antibiotic will be prescribed. Babies tend to be very susceptible to ear infections, and many develop multiple during their time as an infant.

Nose Care

Your baby's nose is likely to get messy, but it should not be hard to clean as long as you handle it right away. For any mucus, clean it gently with a tissue. For anything that is dried up, you should soak a washcloth in warm water to be able to clean it without hurting your baby. They are likely going to squirm when you try to clean their nose, but know that it should not cause them pain, as long as you work gently.

In some cases, using a nasal syringe is necessary. Your baby does not know how to blow their nose, so they can become congested very easily. The nasal syringe consists of a small bulb that works with air pressure to remove any build-up inside of your baby's nose. The nurses at the hospital used this device when your baby was first born. You shouldn't always have to use the nasal syringe, but it is helpful to keep one around just in case.

Diaper Changes and Dressing Baby

Changing your baby's diapers is something that you are going to be able to master efficiently. At first, the concept might be foreign to you, causing you to move slower. Be patient with yourself. You will get better at this the more that you do it. When you suspect that your baby is in need of a diaper change, their behavior will usually confirm this. They might cry or appear visibly uncomfortable. If they have peed in their diaper, it is going to look much denser and have a thicker feel to it from the outside. If your baby has pooped, you are likely going to smell it. You can gently pull back the waistband of the diaper to confirm if your baby has used the bathroom.

Your hygiene matters a great deal when you are changing your baby's diaper. You need to make sure that your hands are washed before you get started. This will ensure that no germs are being spread to your baby. After you finish, of course, you will also wash your hands. When it comes to changing your baby's diaper, you just need to rely on your common sense. Do not use any harsh or perfumed products on your baby that will cause irritation. You will want to be as gentle as you can, too.

Before setting your baby down on the changing pad, make sure that you have your new diaper, wipes, trash can, diaper cream, and any soothing powder at hand. Once you place your baby down on the changing pad, you will not have the opportunity to walk away. After opening your baby's diaper, remove the dirty diaper by gently grabbing both your baby's feet and removing the diaper from underneath them. If your baby has pooped, you can use the upper clean half of the diaper to wipe away the first bit of poop. Then, throw the diaper in the trash.

Take a baby wipe and clean your baby from front to back to avoid infection. You might have to use a couple of wipes if your baby pooped. After ensuring that your baby is fully cleaned, apply any necessary diaper rash cream or powders. Put their new diaper on after this. You will do this by lifting your baby by holding onto their feet gently, and then you will slide their clean diaper underneath them. Once everything has been lined up and adjusted, you can fasten the diaper.

Your baby's diaper should be changed approximately every two to three hours. Of course, this depends on the baby. This gives you a good guideline for how often you should be checking on your baby's diaper, either way. If they are not dirty yet, you can check back again in another hour. Each time that you change your baby's diaper gives you the chance to care for their umbilical cord. Not much needs to be done to it, but you can soak a cotton ball in warm water and wipe away any dry or sticky substances from the perimeter of the cord. After cleaning, pat the area dry with a cloth.

When it comes to changing your baby's clothing, you are going to rely on your common sense again. If your baby soils themselves or gets their clothing dirty in any other way, you can change them to keep them comfortable. Most infant clothing unbuttons or unzips all the way down, allowing you the chance to get their limbs into it easily. If you are putting on a shirt that does not unfasten, place your baby's arms in the armholes gently. You should not have to move your baby into an uncomfortable position to do this. Next, take the hole where their head goes and stretch it out slightly, ensuring that there is plenty of room to put the shirt on without covering your baby's face for a prolonged period of time. This should easily allow you to get their head in the shirt and then straighten up the bottom half of it.

Make sure that your baby's bottoms are not too tight. While the clothing might fit them perfectly, know that a diaper is bulky and it will take up more room. If your baby is experiencing discomfort or fussiness when they wear certain clothing, this might be an indication that you need to size up to give them more room for their crotch and legs. Clothing that is too tight can also lead to diaper rash because of the way that it presses into the skin, so always be cautious about this. You can ensure that your baby's clothing is not too tight if it does not leave any marks on your baby's skin. Marks that outline the stitching are an indication that the clothing is digging into your baby.

Babyproofing

The act of babyproofing involves making your living space a safe space for your baby. While they are an infant, babyproofing might not be one of your largest concerns because they are not yet mobile, but this happens very quickly. Before you know it, they will be crawling around your home and using surfaces to lift themselves into standing positions. It is never too early to implement the appropriate steps of babyproofing so you do not have to worry about them later on. As a new mother, this is going to give you a lot of peace of mind.

Start the process by entering each room individually. This is going to ensure that you do not miss anything. Carefully observe the room you are in and look for any hazards. Once you look around and remove dangerous/sharp/breakable objects, you can sit down on the floor to see things from your baby's perspective. Make sure that you notice things like jagged corners on furniture or accessible electrical outlets. They make devices to pad and protect these areas. You will also want to make sure that your baby cannot accidentally slam their fingers into the door. There are door-stoppers that can prevent this from happening.

Make sure that all of your household chemicals and other toxic substances are kept in a locked cabinet. Babies are very curious and can often accidentally ingest these poisons. The same can be done for any medicines that you have. For anything that can move around, from furniture to objects, it is recommended that you anchor it or remove it when you have a baby. Since they use these things for leverage, they might end up injuring themselves if the item suddenly shifts. It can even fall on top of them, causing another emergency.

All windows must be secured. Make sure that you have screens and appropriate locks in place. Babies love to fidget, and they will not hesitate to try to open things. If your baby ends up prying the windows open, they can end up falling out of them. When you have double measures in place to ensure that this does not happen, you are keeping your baby as safe as possible. Do the same for any doors that lead to the outside, as well. Even if you think your baby cannot reach it, it is better to be safe than sorry.

The way that you cook in the kitchen is also going to experience a transformation. The stove is one of the most dangerous things for your baby to be around. Understandably, there are going to be moments when you must carry or wear your baby while you are cooking. Make sure that you always use the back burners and keep your pots and pans with the handles facing far away from you. Get some guards that you can place over the oven controls to prevent your baby from turning them on. If possible, put your baby in a highchair or other secure chair while you are cooking, this way they can still be with you without being too close to the stove. This isn't always going to be possible, though. If you must hold or carry your baby, use a lot of caution.

Anything that can fall, from your television to home decor, should be double-checked. Make sure that everything is reinforced correctly. As your baby is learning how to crawl and walk, they might end up banging on the walls and surrounding areas. This vibration can cause things to fall from your walls, potentially injuring your baby. If you are unsure if the item is secure, the best decision is to remove it or move it into a different room. Don't forget to test your smoke alarms and carbon monoxide detectors each month, too. These devices are imperative for your baby's safety.

Getting baby gates is going to be something that you should consider, too. While you can do your best to babyproof your entire home, there will likely be some rooms that are safer than others for your baby. You can keep them in these designated rooms with the help of a baby gate. They are secure and still allow your baby to see through them, providing a great barrier between the household dangers and your child. Most gates are adjustable to fit all door frames. This is useful for when you need to bring the gate into other rooms.

While your baby's nursery is obviously one of the safest places for them, you still need to remember to babyproof it. In their crib, make sure that there are no loose blankets or bedding while they sleep. This causes choking or asphyxiation. All outlets in the room need to be covered, and all emergency detectors should be checked on a regular basis. The toys and furniture that you place in the room should not contain any sharp or jagged edges that can hurt your baby. Keep your diaper changing supplies and trash can far away from your baby. They might get curious and try to open up these things.

The car is another place that you need to ensure you babyproof. While there isn't too much you can do, having a proper and safe car seat is the main objective. Not only should you have a great car seat, but you also need to make sure that you know how to install it correctly and how to buckle your baby into it. If necessary, you can get a sunshade that sticks to the glass of the window your baby will be sitting beside. This will prevent overheating. Make sure that you take a baby bag wherever you go in case you need to change your baby, feed your baby, or provide them with some form of entertainment. Getting a "baby on board" sticker is also an option. This sticker alerts medical professionals in case you get into an accident and need assistance.

Bonding

When you have your baby, you are naturally going to expect a wonderful and instantaneous bond with them. This is your child, a part of you that you grew inside of your stomach for nearly a year. It seems obvious that the connection is strong, but this is not always the case. It is normal if your baby does not seem incredibly attached to you at first. Bonding can take time because it is such an individualized process. Do not panic if you feel your baby "doesn't like you." Surely, they do and they will learn how to show it as they develop more ways to do so. This does not make you a bad mother or a terrible parent if your baby does not immediately take to you. Much like yourself, your baby has just been through a very long and confusing process. They need time to get acclimated. Think of your job as their helper, making sure the environment is the best it can possibly be for them. The rest will come naturally.

When your baby is a newborn, you can begin the bonding process by talking to them frequently. While they might not understand exactly what you are saying, babies do have a good grasp of tone. If you use a gentle and friendly tone, your baby is going to remember this and respond well to you. Anything that is too harsh or loud will be apparent by your baby becoming startled or aggravated. It might feel silly to talk to someone who does not respond, but you will see that this changes very quickly. Once your baby starts cooing, it is not a coincidence that they begin making appropriately-timed noises to the things that you say to them.

To bond physically, cuddle with your baby during and after breastfeeding. Once they are done eating, you can burp them and then keep them in your arms for a little cuddle session. This physical closeness is something that quickly bonds a baby to the mother. Both of you will feel a rush of happy hormones that will strengthen your bond each time that you do it. While you are cuddling, you can smile at your baby and make eye contact if they are awake. These gestures are going to become familiar and craved by your little one. They are going to form reassuring feelings that wash over your baby and calm them down.

Whenever you notice that your baby does not feel safe or secure, do everything that you can to change this. While you won't always know what is upsetting them, by constantly showing them that you can make things better, this forms a strong bond of trust. Your baby is counting on you to do these things, and they feel safe when you do them. Don't be too hard on yourself if you cannot fix a problem right away. You are not perfect, and you do not have all of the answers—this is what mothering is all about. Using your instincts, you must discover what is wrong and how to fix it.

As always, your partner should be involved in the bonding process, too. For the one who does not carry and deliver the child, it can seem harder to form a bond, but it is not impossible. Your baby will be familiar with both of you, as long as you both make an effort to become a lasting presence in their life. Get your partner to feed and change the baby as much as you do. Your baby will understand that you are both caretakers. They will see you in the same way, as a source of comfort and safety.

All of the techniques that you use to bond with your baby can also be used by your partner. They can talk to the baby, make eye contact with plenty of smiling, give them cuddles, and more. While the mother does take on a very important role, it is essential that the other parent also feels that they are important. When it comes to bonding with their child, they need to build up their self-confidence by reminding themselves of how important they are. As the mother, you can help with this part by complimenting your partner and reassuring them that they are doing a great job. This makes for a mutually beneficial partnership and a happy baby. Parenting is not a competition. You should not feel like you have to prove yourself to your partner. Instead, you need to work together as a team to do what is best for your baby.

Having Fun as a Family

There are no limits to how much fun you will have one you bring your baby home. This new way of life is going to bring forth so many moments of joy. Getting used to it might take some time, but you should be able to effortlessly attempt these tips of how you can all have fun together as a family:

- **Accept Your Mistakes**: Try not to focus on any parenting mistakes you make—there will be plenty! You are new at this, and you need to offer yourself forgiveness. When you can let go of these mistakes, you will learn from them. This also leaves more room for you to have fun with your family and enjoy the time spent with your baby.

- **Make Silly Faces**: Babies are fascinated by different facial expressions. As their eyesight develops, you might find them smiling or laughing at certain things that you do—own this! Make silly faces at your baby. Not only will this entertain and amuse them, but you will find yourself laughing too.

- **Take Walks**: Going out for a walk is something that you can do with your baby at any age. Get your baby set up in the stroller and enjoy a nice walk. While your baby might end up falling asleep because it is so relaxing, you and your partner can enjoy the sights and get a breath of fresh air.

- **Read Stories Aloud**: Reading to your baby is beneficial in more ways than one. First, it allows them to be soothed by your voice. Hearing your voice is a familiar comfort that never gets old. Second, your baby's brain is rapidly developing. Before you know it, they will be reading you a story. Learning begins during the infant stages, so it is never too early to introduce your baby to new books and stories. They will quickly pick up on these concepts. In the beginning, reading books that also incorporate textures to touch will excite your baby and keep them engaged.

- **Cuddle on the Couch**: When you are watching television, you can bring your baby into the room and cuddle on the couch together. This provides a sense of familial closeness that your baby will feel comforted by. This gives you all the chance to bond as a family while enjoying a moment of downtime. It is also a way for you to reconnect with your partner after a busy day.

- **Get Your Baby Involved**: As you navigate through your daily routine, make sure that you involve your baby whenever possible. As a new mother, you are going to become a narrator. Explain what you are doing and why. This is another way to accelerate your baby's learning. Your baby is very receptive to the things that you do. They will be naturally curious.

- **Play with Toys Together**: Don't just sit your baby down in front of their toys during playtime—get involved! Play with their toys with them. This is going to make the experience feel more fun for them. When they see that you are doing something, this gives them the necessary confidence to feel independent in their own actions.

- **Make Bath Time Fun**: There are plenty of toys that you can give your baby safely while they are bathing. Look into getting some bath toys. This will keep your baby entertained while you wash them, and it will provide a positive connotation with getting in the tub. Many babies are scared of bath time at first, but a couple of toys can easily fix this problem.

- **Do Baby Exercises**: There are ways to help your baby stretch and exercise, even when they are tiny. Look into some appropriate baby exercises and do them frequently. Getting up and moving is a great way for you to stay in shape, and it will also tire your baby out so they sleep wonderfully at night. To a baby, any movement is going to feel exaggerated, so exercise can be exciting.

- **Socialize Often**: When your baby is old enough to meet other people, you can start to bring them around children their own age. This teaches them how to socialize while also introducing them to others. Your baby will naturally gravitate toward certain people based on the feelings that they get. If someone is gentle and nice, your baby will likely feel safe around them. Anyone who is too harsh can scare your baby. When your baby is still too young to talk, observe their facial expressions during social periods. This will tell you everything that you need to know.

Chapter 5:

Baby Health in the First Year

Even as a new mother, your concerns surrounding your baby's health are going to be very strong. It is the one maternal instinct that tends to kick in right away. Whether you are worried about doing the right thing regarding your baby's health or ensuring that your baby does not develop an illness, you are not alone in this feeling. This is motherhood, and you are not going to be able to protect your baby from everything. What you can do, however, is become well-acquainted with what to look for in terms of illnesses that your baby might contract. A lot can happen in your baby's first year of life, but this chapter is meant to get you prepared for it all.

With this experience, you will be able to identify when something is wrong and when to seek medical attention. Making sure that your baby stays healthy is one of the more challenging parts of motherhood, but you are going to feel well-informed after taking a look at each topic. With your newfound confidence, you will be able to protect your baby to the best of your ability.

One of the biggest ways to keep your baby healthy is to keep them happy. If you are meeting all of their essential needs, you are already more than halfway there. The rest comes from being able to recognize the signs and symptoms that something is developing. From there, you will be able to get your baby the proper care that they need.

Baby Vaccines

Your baby will start receiving vaccinations on the day that they are born. Through your baby's first year of life into childhood, they will receive many other vaccinations at your discretion. The following is an example of the typical vaccine schedule and what you can expect from each one. It is important to know exactly what vaccines your baby is being given, as many come with side effects. If you elect to skip a vaccine, you can discuss this decision with your doctor to go over the pros and the cons.

At Birth:

- **HepB**: This vaccine protects your baby against liver infection. It is given in three shots, the first being the same day that your baby is born. This is a vaccine that is typically required by public schools in most states.

Side Effects: Low fever, sore arm from the shot

1-2 Months:

- **HepB**: Once again, it will be time for another hepatitis B vaccine for your baby. This will be the second to last one that they will receive as an infant.

- **RV**: The rotavirus vaccine is typically given to a child in three doses, the first being at around two months. Rotavirus is an infection that causes diarrhea. It is most commonly seen in children under five.

  Side Effects: Irritability, temporary diarrhea, and vomiting

- **DTaP**: The diphtheria, tetanus, and pertussis (whooping cough) is an important vaccine for babies. Since it protects from many illnesses, your baby will need several boosters. It is given in five parts, the first being at around two months.

  Side Effects: Soreness or swelling at the injection site, non-stop crying, and high fever

- **Hib**: This vaccine protects your baby from Influenza type B. This is an infection that is one of the leading causes of bacterial meningitis. It is first given at two months, to be given again three or four times.

Side Effects: Irritability, high fever, loss of appetite, and sleepiness

- **PCV**: The PCV vaccine protects your baby against pneumococcal diseases, such as pneumonia. Very dangerous for your baby if contracted, pneumonia is known for being hard for an infant to fight off. The vaccine is given in four doses, starting at two-months.

Side Effects: Mild fever, loss of appetite, irritability, and sleepiness

- **IPV**: This vaccine protects against polio. Your baby will have their first one at two-months. It will then be given in three more doses of the course of infancy.

Side Effects: Joint pain, body aches, sleepiness, and vomiting

3-6 Months:

- **RV**: Your baby will receive two more boosters for rotavirus. They occur during the fourth month and again during the sixth month.

- **DTaP**: During the fourth month and sixth month, your baby will receive two more boosters of this vaccine.

- **PCV**: It will be time for your baby's boosters. They typically happen during the fourth month and the sixth month.

- **IPV**: Your baby will receive two more doses during their fourth month and their sixth month, with the final dose concluding around four to six years.

- **Influenza**: More commonly known as the flu shot, your baby can have one at around six months. It is a seasonal vaccine that you can opt for yearly from this point on. They are given between September through May.

Side Effects: Low fever, body aches, and soreness at the injection site

6-18 Months:

- **HepB**: Your baby will receive the final hepatitis B booster of their infancy.

- **DTaP**: Your baby will receive their second to last booster of the vaccine. The final one happens at around four-six years.

- **Hib**: Your baby will be due for the second Hib shot at around 12-15 months. This booster is normally given in eight-week intervals from this point, until your baby finishes out the round.

- **PCV**: Your baby will finish out the round at 12-15 months.

- **MMR**: This is a vaccine to protect your baby from measles, mumps, and rubella (German measles). It is given in two doses, the first one occurring between 12-15 months. The second one can be given between four to six years.

Side Effects: Fever, faint red rash, head cold, and sleepiness

- **Varicella**: More commonly known as the chickenpox vaccine, you can get this vaccine for your baby between 12-15 months. It is given in two doses, the final one happening at around four to six years.

Side Effects: Sore arm, mild rash, fever, and temporary stiffness in joints

- **HepA**: A different hepatitis vaccine, your baby will receive their first one at around 12-23 months. The second dose is given six months after the first. HepA is another viral liver disease. It can occur from eating contaminated food or drinking contaminated water.

Side Effects: Low fever, nausea, loss of appetite, and headache

Birth Injuries

It is common to worry about birth injuries that occur when you deliver your baby. Sometimes, medical tools are needed to help get your baby out of the womb. This can involve some pulling and prodding. The good news is that most birth injuries are very minor, and most of them end up healing. Your baby might receive a few scratches, but a lot of them come from their own fingernails as they are getting used to their new range of motion.

If you are worried about birth injuries, have a talk with your delivery team before you go into labor. They will be able to go over what tools might be used and how they are used. This will give you the peace of mind to be able to have a successful delivery without constantly worrying about your baby's health.

For any unanswered questions or concerns, it is always best to consult your doctor. They will be able to provide you with the reassurance that you need. Also, they can give you alternatives to certain procedures that you do not feel comfortable with. Remember, giving birth is a big deal, and you need to be as ready as possible before the moment arrives. Do not feel bad for asking a lot of questions and wanting what is best for your baby—this is already a sign that you are a great mom.

Colic

Discussed in prior chapters, colic is one of the most dreaded potential problems for new mothers. When your baby has colic, they are prone to inconsolable crying. This does not happen for a particular reason, but it can be very upsetting for a parent to deal with. When your baby cries a lot, this leads you to believe that they are unhappy or that you are failing them in some way. Know that colic happens for unknown reasons, so you cannot blame yourself. Some babies just develop it, but they will also outgrow it. Luckily, there are multiple ways that you can deal with it to keep your spirits intact and to comfort your baby to the best of your ability.

The "Five S" Strategy

Swaddling: When you swaddle your baby, they feel more secure. The feeling of their arms being wrapped into the blanket beside their body feels safe. When you swaddle your baby, keep their legs a little looser so they have some wiggle room. You can always try swaddling when you cannot seem to ease your baby's colic.

Shushing: Since your baby is very responsive to sounds, repetitive shushing will likely calm them down.

When inside the uterus, noises can often sound louder than a vacuum cleaner to your little one, but this is what they are used to. This is why babies tend to like white noise and will benefit from having a white noise machine.

Swinging: A slow and steady rocking motion tends to calm a crying infant down. The movement distracts them from their crying. You can also achieve the same effect by placing your baby in a rocking swing or carrier that rocks.

Sucking: During your baby's first few months, they are going to have strong sucking urges. This is natural to them. Once your baby has learned how to latch, you can try offering them a pacifier. This will ease their crying and allow them to give in to their sucking urges.

Side/Stomach: As mentioned earlier, the colic carry is very beneficial because it allows your baby to have some time on their side or stomach. Placing them across your lap with their head in your hands, this position seems to put infants with colic at ease.

Each baby is different, but you can try all of the steps of the "Five S" method to soothe your little one. Colic will subside eventually, so you just have to do your best to ease the tears in the meantime. Don't give up or feel disappointed. This is something many mothers experience with their babies, and your doctor will likely have some words of encouragement for you if you are feeling lost.

When your baby has a lot of gas, this will often lead to colic. To prevent gas from building up, make sure that your baby is being burped properly and that they are using the bathroom enough. You can also try giving them soft stomach massages to loosen up the gas. If you are breastfeeding, you can also look into changing your diet to reflect a healthier menu. What you ingest is being fed to your baby, too.

Vomiting

Vomiting is a very common issue when you have an infant. When your baby vomits, this does not necessarily mean that they have an illness. Sometimes, your baby will vomit after eating too much, but it is important to recognize the difference between vomiting and spitting up.

Vomiting: A forceful regurgitation

Spitting Up: A dribble that flows from the mouth

Some of the most common causes of vomiting found in infants include:

- Gas
- Food allergies
- Infections
- Appendicitis

Most often, the vomiting is going to be gas-related, but it does help to know when to contact your doctor. After your baby vomits, keep a close eye on them. As you are monitoring them, check to see if they are running a fever. With a fever and vomiting combined, it is recommended to contact your doctor right away. This can be a sign of a more serious illness or infection.

If your baby still feels well enough to eat and play, the vomiting is likely a temporary occurrence that will pass. You know your baby best, so you will be able to tell if they do not seem like themselves. If they are feeling irritable or less responsive to your actions, it is recommended that you contact your doctor.

When the vomiting gets to the point where your little one cannot stop and can no longer hold down liquids, you will need to visit urgent care or the ER. Vomiting is a leading cause of dehydration, and if your baby is not keeping their fluids down, they are not going to be able to be replenished correctly.

The most important thing for you to do as a mother is to stay calm. Observe your baby, and use your knowledge to decide on what you need to do next. Panicking is only going to make your baby feel more panicked. If you can stay calm and assess the situation, you will be able to do what is best for your baby.

Fever

There are many ways that you can tell if your baby is experiencing a fever, and this extends beyond them feeling hot to the touch. A fever can happen for many reasons, from a cold to a more serious infection. No matter what the underlying cause is, you can observe your baby for the following signs:

- **Shivering**: When your baby has a fever, it can come in stages. One stage is when they appear shivery and cold on the outside. This behavior will be noticeably unusual, and you should use a thermometer to take your baby's temperature. If your baby does have a high temperature, you might need to change your baby's clothing to make sure that they are warm and comfortable enough. Make sure that the room they are in is well-ventilated, and encourage them to rest.

- **Appearing Hot and Flushed**: This is the most common way to notice if your baby has a fever. Their cheeks will appear pink and their forehead will be hot to the touch. Using the back of your hand, you can touch their forehead and cheeks to determine if they are feeling feverish. As always, you can use a thermometer to confirm their temperature. Keep your baby comfortable and give them plenty of fluids to keep them hydrated.

- **Irritability**: Your baby will go through irritable spells, but you know them best. Trust your instincts if you notice that your baby is feeling fussier than usual. Their cry might also sound different to you. Keep an eye on them after you notice this increased irritability because a fever might be soon to follow. There is no harm in visiting your doctor if you can't seem to pinpoint exactly what is wrong.

- **A High Temperature**: A fever of 100.4-degrees is considered very high for babies. If you notice that their temperature has reached this level, it is recommended that you get them to a doctor right away. Anything under this temperature should be closely monitored.

- **Loss of Appetite**: If your baby doesn't seem interested in eating or drinking as much as usual, they might not be feeling well. Because you have a schedule in place, you will notice right away when your little one seems to deviate. If this behavior becomes concerning, bring it up to your doctor.

There are certain illnesses that babies tend to develop that will lead to fevers. Some of them include ear infections, colds, flu, roseola (a viral illness), and throat infections. After you have visited the doctor regarding your baby's fever and potential illness, your goal should be to keep them as comfortable as possible. Give them plenty of cuddles and encourage napping. Depending on what is going on, your baby might be prescribed an antibiotic that makes them sleepy or causes them to lose their appetite. Do your best to keep them well-fed and hydrated.

Ear Infections

Babies are prone to ear infections because they often stem from having runny noses. Catching a common cold is normal for an infant because their immune system is still developing. Babies who are around other babies tend to have a higher risk of exposure because ear common colds are so contagious. In some cases, ear infections can also develop because they run in the family. While they can be frustrating to deal with, know that they are fairly easy to handle with the help of your doctor. The most common symptoms include nasal congestion, nasal discharge, ear pain or pulling, temporary hearing loss, ear discharge, fever, or fussiness.

An antibiotic is normally required, but you will have to consult your doctor first. If you do receive antibiotics for your baby, and they do not feel better within three to four days, you will need to follow-up with your doctor. In addition, a follow-up will be needed as soon as your baby finishes the course of the antibiotic treatment plan. Your baby can have repeated ear infections, but they shouldn't be a cause of concern as long as they heal completely in between. Having four ear infections within six months, or six within twelve is a sign that an Ear, Nose, and Throat specialist should be contacted.

To prevent ear infections from occurring, breastfeed for as long as possible. Try to breastfeed your baby for the first three months of their life to strengthen their immune system. Vaccinating your child for pneumonia and the flu can help to decrease their chances of developing an ear infection. Most children outgrow getting ear infections between three to five years. To treat your baby's ear infection at home, you can use the following tips:

- **Warm Compress**: Soak a washcloth in warm water and then wring it out. Place this warm compress over your baby's ears to relieve the pain and pressure.
- **Elevation**: By keeping your baby's head elevated, this can alleviate your baby's pain and prevent any nasal discharge from draining into your baby's ear canals.
- **Oil Treatment**: Warm up some olive oil and carefully play it into your baby's ears. You can use a dropper or a cotton swab to apply it. The oil can alleviate the pain.
- **Tylenol (for babies over six months)**: Painkillers can be used to help with some of the

milder symptoms. Follow the appropriate dosage options for your baby's age.

In some cases, your baby's ear infections can get better on their own. If they do not have a fever and the pain seems only mild, the ear infection might go away on its own. Over time, your baby will most likely learn how to heal from ear infections if they get them more than once.

Skin Problems

Your baby's skin is very fragile. It is prone to many different skin issues, but the good news is that most of them are easy to resolve. The following are some that you might encounter during your baby's infancy and how to treat them:

- **Cradle Cap**: Cradle cap appears as a crusty, almost scaly, texture on your baby's scalp. It is something similar to dandruff in adults. This is a very common condition for infants up to three months. It is caused by surges of hormones, and not all babies will develop it. Not much can be done, as the cradle cap is nothing more than harmless dry skin that will go away eventually. If you do want to treat it, you can use petroleum jelly on your baby's scalp. Make sure that you thoroughly shampoo and rinse your baby's hair during bathtime, as any residual product will cause more build-up.

- **Infant Eczema**: Eczema is an itchy rash that tends to start on your baby's face. It can then spread to their body. The rash appears as small, fluid-filled pimples that can burst or ooze. To ease the pain for your baby, you can apply a hypoallergenic moisturizer to eczema. You can also run a cool-mist humidifier in the nursery. In some cases, your doctor will prescribe a prescription cream to treat the rash.

- **Dry Skin**: This is a very common skin condition that your baby will likely experience. Everyone gets dry skin at times, but babies are especially prone to it due to their new skin cells. The best way to combat this is by keeping your baby hydrated and using hypoallergenic moisturizer. If you notice the dry skin worsening, you might need to cut down on bathtime, as soaking in the water dries out your baby's skin more.

- **Bottom Rashes**: Diaper rash can occur no matter how clean you keep your baby and no matter how frequently you change them. This painful rash burns and makes your baby fussy for good reason. The best thing that you can do is to thoroughly wipe your baby during diaper changes and apply safe diaper cream to the areas where they are experiencing the rash.

- **Heat Rashes/Sunburn**: Heat rash can happen due to sun exposure because of clogged pores. Sunburn is also a valid concern because of your baby's skin sensitivity. When you do take your baby outside, make sure to apply plenty of infant sunblock. Also, dress them in protective clothing and keep them in the shade as much as possible. If your baby does get sunburnt or experiences heat rash, you can use a cool compress to ease the pain. If any vomiting occurs, contact your doctor immediately because there is a risk of sun poisoning.

- **Insect Bites**: If your baby spends time outside, they are likely to get bitten by insects. This is one of the most common skin problems that you will deal with as an infant. No treatment is necessary unless you notice your baby's skin swelling and reddening around the bite. This can be an indication that they are allergic to the insect. Your doctor will be able to advise if an Epi-pen is needed, but most of the time, a Benadryl cream for babies will do.

Other Concerns

- **Teething**: As your baby grows, teething is something that you will inevitably have to deal with. Your baby's mouth will become sore, causing them to get fussy. You can give them teething toys that are freezable. The coolness will feel great on their gums, and it will give them something to safely chew on.

- **Oral Thrush**: This is like a yeast infection, but it happens inside of your baby's mouth. It is noticeable by its yellow patches on your baby's gums, sides of the mouth, and roof of the mouth. It often goes away on its own in a few days' time, but an antifungal medication provided by your doctor can help. You can also put it on your nipples if your baby is breastfeeding.

- **Diarrhea/Constipation**: There will be times when your baby has trouble pooping. Whether the poop is too loose or too hard, babies have very delicate stomachs. You can help your baby by giving them plenty of gentle stomach massages and moving their legs in a circular motion. A warm bath can also help them relax enough to poop successfully.

- **Coughing**: If your baby is coughing with no fever, make sure that their nasal passages are clear. Use a cool-mist humidifier in the nursery to help them breathe better. You can also promote them to drink plenty of liquids, such as milk, juice, and water. If the coughing persists, you might have to visit your doctor for some medicine.

- **Abdominal Distention**: If you notice that your baby has been constipated for days and has a hard abdomen, they might be experiencing abdominal distention. The most likely cause is constipation or gas, but consult your doctor if you cannot get your baby to poop. This can be a very painful experience for them because they are not getting any relief.

Chapter 6:

Postpartum Depression:

The Dark Secret of

Motherhood

As a new mother, you only hear about the joys of motherhood. You hear about what it feels like to meet your baby for the first time, the bond that you have. What happens when your experience is not like this at all? Maybe you deliver your baby, only to realize that you are very depressed, not connected to anyone or anything. If this happens to you, know that this is a normal condition experienced by many mothers all over the world. This is postpartum depression, and it is a common condition for new moms to develop. No matter how much you have been looking forward to having your baby, the postpartum depression can still rise to the surface before you realize what is happening.

There is not only a single reason why you might develop the condition, but there are a few prominent factors. Hormones can have something to do with it.

After you give birth, your estrogen levels and progesterone levels experience a big drop. When you have been living with elevated levels for nearly a year, your body gets used to this. As these hormones drop, your thyroid function can also drop. This is what leaves you feeling depressed and sluggish. Changes in your blood pressure, immune system, and metabolism can all trigger your experience with postpartum depression, as well.

On a physical level, your body has undergone very big physical changes since giving birth to your baby. You might be dealing with this pain, wondering if everything is going to be back to normal soon. As you settle into your new normal, it can feel like a never-ending cycle. Because of this, you might no longer feel physically or sexually attractive. It is a hard realization to face, especially when you and your partner are so focused on welcoming the new baby into your home. Your needs and desires are put onto the back burner.

Stress is another factor that makes a big difference in your life. With a new baby, your stress levels will naturally increase. There is going to be a lot of crying, a lot of waking up in the middle of the night for feedings. This experience is a lot different than being able to carry your baby in the womb and supply all their needs. As a first-time mother, you are likely still grasping your new identity. Because you have not been doing this for a long time, it makes sense that you might question your ability to take care of your newborn, causing you to feel inadequate.

Those who have experienced non-pregnancy related depression are more likely to face postpartum depression. Having a family history of mood disorders can also impact your own experience after you give birth. Just because you have experienced depression in the past does not mean that you will automatically suffer from postpartum depression, but it doesn't hurt to prepare for the possibility. Some other factors that can contribute to your development include a lack of emotional support during your pregnancy, an abusive relationship, financial uncertainty, and other social stressors. Another thing to keep in mind is if you discontinue taking any medication abruptly after finding out that you were pregnant. Women who do this have a significantly increased risk of developing postpartum depression.

What is the Difference Between PPD and Baby Blues?

A common condition that mothers develop after pregnancy is the baby blues. This differs from postpartum depression (PPD) because it is not as serious. Immediately after childbirth, it is common for the new mother to experience at least a little bit of baby blues. This does have something to do with the sudden change in hormones in your body, but it also can be combined with the stress that was experienced during delivery. After giving birth, everything seems to be moving very quickly for you and your new baby. You might feel like you don't have the chance to just sit and relax with your little one, causing you to feel overwhelmed and fatigued. Don't worry because this is bound to change very soon. Once you get used to your routine, you will usually be able to beat the baby blues.

When you have the baby blues, you might feel extra emotional in the days to follow your delivery. This can mean more tearful moments and more emotional fragility. Know that this is perfectly normal. You can probably compare the feeling of having the baby blues to having some severe PMS symptoms. Much like the latter, the others will also go away on their own. You will notice a peak in these symptoms after one week postpartum, but then you can expect them to taper off by the time that you enter the second week. This is a good indication that what you are experiencing is the baby blues. It should not last much longer than this. If it does, you might need to consult your doctor to determine if you are suffering from PPD.

You can think of the baby blues as mild depression, whereas PPD is more severe depression. When you have mild depression, mood swings are still common. One moment, you might be happy to be spending time with your baby and your family, and then that feeling will subside and become replaced with stress or anxiety. This is new for you, so don't forget to give yourself plenty of time to breathe. Needing a break does not make you a bad or weak mom. Make sure that your partner is playing an equal role to prevent either one of you from feeling burnt out. Your partner can help you a lot during times when you feel that you have the baby blues. By picking up the slack, you won't be left feeling quite so overwhelmed.

What Are Recognizable Symptoms?

PPD is something that should not go ignored. Because it is a more intense form of depression than the baby blues, you might need to consult your doctor for a solution. When you have PPD, you will experience a wide range of symptoms. A couple of these things are what you can also experience when you have the baby blues, but the difference is that they are more severe when you are dealing with PPD. Pay attention to the severity of each symptom that you feel, and see if you can relate to these. Some of the most common symptoms are the following:

- **Withdrawing**: After giving birth, you probably imagined that you would feel closer to your new family than ever before. Every moment leading up to the delivery showed you that you would be spending plenty of time enjoying your baby and bonding with your partner over the new arrival. If things do not go as planned, you might be experiencing symptoms of withdrawal.

  No matter who you are withdrawing from, your baby, or your partner, this is a sign that PPD might be occurring. If you feel that you cannot bond with your baby or that you are no longer close with your partner, know that this feeling will pass with the proper treatment. There is nothing wrong with you or nothing about you that is causing the bonding to feel this way.

- **Anxiety**: When you have anxiety that is out of control, it will impact you both mentally and physically. You might not be able to eat or sleep, and this makes it much more difficult to take care of your baby. In order to provide them with nourishment, you need to be taking the best care of yourself, as well. Your mind will run wild with the what-ifs, torturing you into thinking that you aren't doing a good job.

  Even when your baby appears fine, like when they are eating or sleeping, you might be second-guessing yourself and wondering why you are doing everything wrong. This type of anxiety can place a lot of unrealistic expectations on you, preventing you from enjoying this time that you have with your newborn.

- **Guilt**: After you give birth to your baby, you might experience a feeling of being washed over by guilt. This can be incredibly difficult to manage when you have a newborn baby that needs your care. You might feel guilty over how you delivered your baby or how much you can give them now that they are born. These thoughts will keep cycling through your mind, making you preoccupied.

When you have intense guilt, this can make even the most enjoyable moments stressful because you are constantly worrying. In most cases, it is easy enough to move past the guilt and focus on the positive sides, but PPD makes this part difficult. This might prove to be a feeling that you cannot shake.

- **Worthlessness**: It can be very hard to experience worthlessness when you have a new baby to care for. They are depending on you for everything from nourishment to shelter. On the inside, all you might be able to feel is that your life no longer matters. On some days, you might even wish that you could just disappear altogether.

  This reaction tends to come with the fact that you are already very stressed out. Raising a baby is not easy, but this does not mean that you are worthless because you are trying your best. No mother has all of the answers, so you should not expect yourself to have them.

- **Suicidal Thoughts**: One of the most serious symptoms of PPD is suicidal thoughts. Just because you have PPD does not automatically mean that you will develop these thoughts, but it is important that you look out for them. Becoming preoccupied with death, or wanting to die, is very dangerous and should be reported to a medical professional right away. If you are experiencing this, do not delay telling someone and getting help.

The sooner you open up to someone you trust, the sooner you will be able to feel relief from all of your PPD symptoms. Motherhood is not all stress and worry. You will get the hang of it, and you will be able to enjoy your life in your new role. Lean on your partner for extra support, when necessary. Look at your baby, remembering that you brought them into this world. You completed a huge task already, and you are wonderful for doing so.

Best Coping Strategies

There are ways to cope with your PPD, no matter how severe it gets. When you prioritize taking care of your baby, this automatically means that you must take care of yourself. What you can provide for your baby is a direct extension of what you can provide for yourself. While this time is going to be difficult for you, know that this is not what it will feel like forever. You have the strength to get through this, and you can do so by trying some of these coping strategies:

1. **Create a Secure Attachment**: Known as an attachment, this is the emotional bonding process that occurs between you and your baby. To create a secure attachment, you have to pay attention to your baby. When they are feeling discomfort, try to soothe them right away. After they start crying, offer them solutions, whether they are cuddles or feeding.

    Your baby is going to feel secure when they know that you are always there for them. It is a way to build trust that your baby is going to understand, even as an infant. This is how you are going to set yourself up for a great relationship with your baby as they grow older. It will also show you that you have plenty of purpose and reason to be there, as PPD can often trick you into feeling otherwise.

2. **Lean on Others for Help**: No matter what you are going through, you don't have to keep your feelings to yourself. If you don't want to admit exactly how you are feeling to your partner, consider opening up to another mother. You would be surprised at how many other mothers in your life have also dealt with PPD and successfully overcame it.

Even if you don't want to go very in-depth, it helps to have emotional support. Raising a child is a big responsibility, and that is going to come with a lot of questions and concerns. Anyone who appears supportive in your life right now should be someone you are spending time with. Don't forget to prioritize these relationships in your life.

3. **Take Care of Yourself**: After you give birth, you shouldn't have to jump back into doing all of the housework. Let your partner take care of this, as you need to take care of your body. While the first thing you might want to do is make the house as perfect as possible, you need to put yourself first. Make sure that you are fully healed before you get back into any kind of physical activity. You are already going to be moving around a lot to tend to your baby.

When you do start feeling better in a few weeks, you can get back into low-impact exercise. This involves walking and doing gentle at-home workouts. The endorphin rush will help you combat your PPD. By exercising, you will also be getting better sleep at night. This is essential for any new parent. If you need additional time to clear your head, practice some mindfulness meditation.

4. **Make Time for Your Partner**: The time that you used to spend with your partner has now

been filled with ways to take care of your infant—this is natural, but you don't want to let your little one take over every single opportunity that you get with your partner. Keep your relationship strong during this time. You will both need mutual support.

When your baby is asleep, check-in with your partner. See how they are doing and what they are feeling. You both know the experience best, as you are raising the same child. Being able to talk to someone who can relate to you might provide you with some relief. Plus, it will keep your bond close. Don't forget to engage in intimate moments together. Even if you don't feel like having sex yet, cuddling, kissing, and hugging are all great ways to re-enter the intimacy.

5. **Seek Professional Help**: If you feel that you cannot handle your PPD on your own, commend yourself by taking the big step of getting help. Your doctor will be able to help you in a few ways. One of which is attending individual therapy or marriage counseling. Talking to a professional can be enough to ease your mind. When you can get the worrisome things off your chest, you are making more room for happiness.

Antidepressants or hormone therapy might also be recommended to you. No matter which is recommended, your doctor will be keeping a close eye on you to make sure that you are reacting well to the medication and that you are safe. Each option has its own set of risks that will have to be reviewed thoroughly before you decide to take anything.

Seeking Medical Treatment

If you suspect that your postpartum depression is getting too hard for you to manage, do not hesitate to talk to your doctor. When you are open about your feelings, your doctor will be able to make an official diagnosis. Through your evaluation, your doctor will be able to determine if you are experiencing the short-term impacts of the baby blues or the long-term suffering that comes with PPD. No matter your diagnosis, know that there is help readily available to you. When you decide to get help with your PPD, this does not make you a bad mother. It makes you a great one because you can acknowledge that you need some help before you can be the very best for your baby.

An evaluation for PPD is not something that should be scary or concerning to you. Once you get to your doctor's office, you will likely be given a questionnaire to fill out. This will include questions about depression and symptoms relating to it. Make sure that you are as honest as possible during this screening because this is what your doctor will go off of. There is no need to feel like keeping up appearances in the doctor's office because you are there to get help. As you answer each question, go with your first instinct and be as honest as possible.

Your doctor might order a blood test at your appointment. This can showcase any thyroid problems that you might be having, which can contribute to your PPD. An underactive thyroid can typically be treated with medication. This will balance your body out again and allow the correct hormones to flow through your system. When you do not have the right hormones to get through each day, this will be reflected in the level of severity of your PPD. Know that your body does or does not produce these hormones naturally and that this isn't your fault. If you had the choice, you know that you would not resort to PPD.

If your doctor sees anything else that they want to take a look at, more tests can be ordered. This is all that you can expect from the typical appointment to diagnose PPD, though. The treatment methods and recovery times will vary based on your doctor's recommendation. They are going to take your specific situation into account and do what will work best for you. PPD is normally treated with psychotherapy, or talk therapy. This gives you a one-on-one experience with a therapist to talk through your recent feelings and behaviors since having your baby. It might also be beneficial to do a few sessions with your partner if you two are experiencing difficulties due to your PPD.

Much like the questionnaire that you were given at your initial appointment, you need to be as honest as possible if you do enter some form of talk therapy. The therapist is not there to pass any judgments. They are simply there to listen and to help you find ways through your difficult situations. When you lie to your therapist, you are only creating more work for yourself to complete in the future. Think about your baby and how you want to get better. When you set a concrete focus, you will be met with great results that you can feel proud of.

Alternatively, you might be prescribed some medication to help you with your PPD. Antidepressants work well for PPD because they assist with other types of severe depression. While there are naturally going to be risks involved when starting a new medication, you can ask your doctor to walk you through all of the side effects before you decide if you want to go with the given recommendation. Keep in mind that breastfeeding makes it possible for your medication to enter breast milk. While most medications can safely enter your bloodstream without any negative impacts to your baby, it is best to tell your doctor that you are breastfeeding and that you want an antidepressant with few side effects.

Treating your PPD is important because it can turn into chronic depression if left untreated. The same can be said about stopping treatment too early. If you get diagnosed with PPD by your doctor and given a treatment plan, make sure that you take this seriously. Getting past your PPD is possible, as long as you follow all of the instructions given by your doctor. When you have found an appropriate treatment plan, you should feel your symptoms easing off. While you aren't going to be bright and happy overnight, there should be a little improvement that suggests what you are doing is working.

Postpartum Psychosis

Postpartum psychosis is incredibly rare, but it is a condition that can happen to new mothers who have just given birth. This condition differs from PPD because postpartum psychosis causes you to lose touch with reality. There is a very high risk of suicide and infanticide in those who suffer from PPP. For this reason, a hospital stay is likely required to help the mother exit this state of being. The condition can develop suddenly, therefore, not many are able to exhibit any warning signs that suggest they need help. During the first two weeks following delivery is when a new mother will be most susceptible to PPP, but it can happen as soon as two hours after delivery. These are some of the most common symptoms:

- Hallucinations
- Delusions
- Extreme agitation and anxiety
- Suicidal thoughts or actions
- Confusion and disorientation

- Rapid mood swings
- Bizarre behavior
- Irritability
- Refusal to eat or sleep
- Thoughts of harming or killing your baby

While all of these symptoms might sound outlandish to you now, you are not going to understand that you are going through them if they happen to you. This is why it is important for your partner to be aware of postpartum psychosis, too. When they are just as informed as you are, they will know when a medical professional needs to be contacted, and when you might need additional help. PPP is a scary condition to develop, but it can pass effectively given the correct treatment plan.

This condition is seen as a medical emergency that should be taken seriously. Even if you can feel that something is not right with you, yet you don't want to exaggerate, it is better to get evaluated than to leave that feeling lingering within. Giving birth is a very taxing and emotional experience. It takes time for your life to get back to normal after you give birth to your baby, but this transition should be smooth and gradual. If anything ever feels rushed or scary, then you might be having a hard time coping with it. Just because PPP is rarer than PPD does not mean that no one else can relate to its struggles. There are plenty of mothers who reach this state of psychosis and are able to come out of it on the other side.

When reading about this condition, you do not need to try and scare yourself to prevent this from happening to you. Since it is a mental illness, it can be brought on at any time. The purpose of getting informed is to be as prepared as possible. As you will quickly learn, preparing for things ahead of time is one thing that makes motherhood a lot easier. This includes any issues that you might deal with yourself. Always prepare for the worst, but don't get too caught up on what to do next until you start exhibiting the symptoms. Inform yourself of what to do, and make this a learning experience that you can share with your partner.

If it helps, you can do your research on other mothers who have experienced the condition. By reading about first-hand accounts of PPP, this might put things into a better perspective for you. Not only will you be able to compare your feelings, but you will also get the chance to see if what you are feeling lines up with the feelings of those who have suffered from PPP. Keeping your mind occupied with your baby and your new life can help. As long as you aren't having any dangerous thoughts, stay focused on how to make your baby happy and your happiness will usually follow.

Do not spend too much time worrying about PPP, or else it will end up taking over your mind in a different way. The only things that are worth focusing on when you have an infant are the things that will help them learn and grow. You need to set your sights on doing what is best for your baby and how you can do your best to take care of them. Your partner will help you watch for the right symptoms, and if you begin to show them, then you can be evaluated by a medical professional for an official diagnosis. Never assume that you have PPP without talking to a doctor first.

Chapter 7:

Keeping Your Relationship

Stable After the Birth of

Your Child

After you have your baby, this is not the only recognizable change that you will experience in your household. Since the two of you became parents, you might find that you and your partner experience some relationship changes, too. Being a parent places you into a different role than you have ever been in before. This now means that you are completely responsible for another human life. That is a lot of pressure to handle on a daily basis, and it comes complete with its fair share of trial and error. While you know that being a mother takes time to master, so does being a father. If you can stay mindful of this, you can continue to make sure that your relationship with your partner is strong and wonderful.

More than ever, the two of you are going to have to work together as a team. From caring for the baby to making decisions that will impact the baby, being parents really makes you work together in every aspect of life. This can be a lot on some relationships that never had to incorporate this type of partnership into their dynamic before. You are likely to learn a lot about one another, even if you have been together for a long time prior to having a baby. Be patient with one another as you go because neither one of you is perfect. By working together, you can help each other be the best you can be.

Work as a Team

Establish that both of you are going to feel incredibly exhausted. This should never become a competition. Being able to respect one another when you are both very tired is a big challenge that you are going to have to learn how to deal with. There is no working around the exhausting parts of parenting an infant. This is only a stage that is temporary, though. Practice your patience now more than ever, just as your partner did when you weren't feeling well during your pregnancy. Your tempers might be shorter than ever, but remember that working together is going to get you where you need to be rather than working against each other and fighting.

While your baby might be too little to understand what certain words mean, they are still going to pick up on your tone and attitude. If a baby's parents are always fighting or not getting along, they are going to feel the residual effects of this. If you do have a disagreement that you need to sort through, have a talk about it when you can be alone. If you are always talking negatively around your baby, this kind of energy will be likely to upset them. If you stay mindful about what is important, there should be very few things that you are not able to discuss in front of your baby. You need to use your problem-solving skills as a couple to reach this point together.

If something goes wrong, refrain from blaming one another. This is only going to fuel the fire and make you both even more upset. What needs to happen is for the two of you to come together as a couple and decide what needs to change to prevent the same thing from happening again. This is where the trial and error comes in. Neither one of you can assume that the other knows exactly what they are doing. You both read the same literature before your baby arrived, and now you need to put it to the test.

When something goes wrong with a parenting decision, it is natural to look for a scapegoat to blame. This isn't the healthiest way to handle these situations, though. You might be at-fault, but that doesn't mean you are a bad mother. Admit to your mistakes, and this will show your partner that it is okay to admit to theirs, too. When you can let go of the image of perfection that seems to fill your mind before you have your baby, you will be able to see things clearer. There is no need to find someone or something else to blame, but there is a need to brainstorm ideas on how to make things better in the future.

If you do end up reacting harshly toward your partner, know that you should not be above apologizing. Giving your partner a heartfelt apology can ease tensions and allow you to work well together again. It can be very difficult to admit when you have done something wrong, but this is a great quality to possess. It shows that you are only human and that you make mistakes sometimes. Delivering an apology is like a form of intimacy, in a way. It is unique to the situation that is going on, and it should come from your heart. This is how you are going to get your partner to forgive you so you can both move on.

You and your partner are likely together nearly 24/7. Wherever the baby is, you both will be. This can cause a lot of tension in your relationship, especially when you were used to going to your own separate jobs and having some space from one another. During this time, you are going to be seeing a lot of each other, so it is okay to request some alone time. This does not mean that you must be mad at each other, but it shows that you can have a healthy sense of boundaries in your relationship. Know that you do not have to do every single thing together, but some things are more beneficial when you can both do them, like taking turns feeding your little one. If you need some time to unwind by yourself, just listen to your instincts.

If there is an ongoing issue that needs resolution, sit down with your partner, and have a mature conversation about it. Your baby should not be the center of attention in this discussion, as you know what arguing or talking intensely around a baby can do.

Prepare your points and express why you believe in the particular cause that you are arguing. Together, you should be able to come up with solutions that please both of you. Aim to keep talking until you can come to a conclusion that feels resolved. Anything that gets left hanging is bound to come up again in the near future.

Prepare for Changes

After finding out that you are expecting a baby, you should know that your relationship dynamic as a couple is going to change. There will be fewer moments of spontaneity. If the joy in your relationship stems from spontaneous decisions, you are going to have to regroup as a couple. It is hard to be impulsive when you have a newborn baby. They have their own needs and desires that must be tended to before your own. You will no longer be able to pack up and get in the car on a whim because this can be enough to cause your baby to feel alarmed. Be prepared to turn down any last-minute invitations to hang out with your friends, as well. These are just some of the things that will change when you become a parent.

During moments of free time, you were likely able to focus on the romance that you share as a couple. Now, the focus will be on your baby. Getting alone time usually means that you will end up discussing your baby or how things are going. It takes a lot more effort to enter the romantic side of your relationship after your baby is born, but it is not impossible. Make sure that you still tell your partner how much they mean to you. Try to get back some of that original chemistry that you felt when you first met one another. It still exists, but it might just need some coaxing to uncover. Try your best to keep up with regular date nights, even leaving your house seems like the last thing you want to do.

Because of what you have just been through physically, the desire to have sex might also be limited. Sex is something that tends to connect couples in a way that nothing else can, but you can expect it to become lower on the list of priorities that you have after you become parents. Not only are you going to be healing and tired, but you might also feel too busy to include sex into your daily routine. Don't be too hard on yourselves in the beginning; you need time to adjust to the new schedule. As long as you keep the romance alive, the sex life will return as well. When you are able to get rid of any expectations that surround sex, you will be able to incorporate it back into your life naturally.

There is also the financial aspect of your life as a couple that you need to handle after you have a baby. You are going to need to purchase a lot more things for your little one, as well as give up a few things that you used to buy for yourself because you had the money to spare. Saving up your money before you have a baby is a wise decision because you never know when you might need to buy something unexpectedly. An unplanned doctor's visit might set you back financially. You can save up your money by cutting down on unnecessary expenses before your baby arrives. For example, you can forgo the regular trips to the salon if it means being able to put money into your baby's fund each month.

For the first few months after you bring your baby home, you and your partner are likely going to feel like you are both running a tag-team race that doesn't end. Because you are the main two in the race, the duties get passed on to one another like a baton. Make sure that you are not treating your new life as parents like too much of a business transaction. Remember that you two are still the same people who fell in love with one another. Keep the fun present by remembering to include humor into your daily tasks. You do not have to take everything so seriously now just because you are parents. Being able to lighten up and have some fun will make things feel less robotic.

While your baby is going to feel like the very center of your world for a few months, do not forget that you still have needs that are not related to parenting. You might crave intimacy while your partner craves alone time. Make sure that you discuss these things and know what the other person is expecting from the relationship at this time. Part of having a healthy relationship means being able to openly discuss your needs without feeling guilty or embarrassed.

Handling Jealousy

Jealousy will come naturally when a couple has a baby. This is not surprising because your partner did not have the chance to carry your baby in the womb for nine months. While biology cannot change, you can do your best to make your partner feel included. From the moment that your baby is born, it is understandable that you would not want to let them go. You have just spent so long carrying them, and finally, delivering them. Remember that your partner has been waiting for all of this time, too. They are equally excited to meet your little one, and they would like their own chance to bond.

Sometimes, you have to let your baby go, even when you don't feel like it. Just as it is important to have a healthy bond with your baby, it is also important for your partner to have the same bond. This is how a baby grows up having two happy parents in a secure household. In turn, try not to experience jealousy when you see that the baby is taking to your partner. You should view this as a great thing because this means that they are bonding successfully, and this is bringing even more joy to your baby's life.

When your baby goes to sleep, this is your chance as a couple to come together. If you are both home, use this time to catch-up with one another. While you might always be around each other and taking care of the baby, there is seldom time to talk about your feelings.

Be open and honest with each other; it is better than holding everything in. As new parents, you cannot necessarily predict when you will get alone time together, but you should be able to take advantage of the time that you do get.

If you don't have anything serious to talk about, use this time to just be with one another and enjoy each other's company. Who says you can't have a mini-date while your baby naps? As you know, keeping the romance alive is a very important priority to have as a couple with a new baby. This will remind you that you aren't only parents; you are also two individuals with needs and desires. Remember what you liked to do before you became parents and how you would act on your needs for intimacy.

Experiencing jealousy does not make you a bad parent. It is a natural feeling to have when you have just had a baby. Instead of punishing yourself for feeling this way, or shutting down, speak up about the issue. Your partner will probably understand because they have likely also experienced their own moments of jealousy. When you get everything out in the open, the two of you will probably be able to laugh about it and come to a solution. This is what open communication will do for you.

If your jealousy issues start causing serious fights, then you know that something must change in your daily routine. Someone is feeling left out, and this should be taken seriously. You are a family unit, and you should be able to operate together. If one person is feeling left out, think about ways that you can do more together, or even things that they can do alone with the baby. You need to put your trust in your partner and know that they are the baby's other parent. While they do not have the same maternal instincts that you have, they do have their very own set. Trust in them as they trusted in you to bring a healthy baby into the world. You didn't know what you were doing at first, but you adapted and succeeded. Believe that they can do the same while bonding with the baby.

Working on Intimacy

The best way to work on your intimacy as a couple who just had a baby is to not place pressure on the idea of having sex right away. This pressure worsens when one of you is in the mood, but the other is just not there yet. You need to be patient with each other because the feelings will return. On your behalf, think about what your body has just been through. It is okay if you don't feel sexy immediately after giving birth, but this is your chance to be with your partner and engage in other intimate actions that will bring your confidence back. Kissing, hugging, and cuddling are all great forms of intimacy that you can start with. Just because you aren't having sex yet doesn't mean that you cannot do all of the above in abundance. Get back into the mood by being physical in any way you can.

Talking about your desires can help you as a couple. Think back to when you first started dating—you were both likely more vocal about your wants and needs. Get back to this space and share openly with one another. It might feel a little bit foreign at first, but remember who you are talking to. This is the person that you are spending your life with and raising a family with. They want to please you just as much as you want to please them. For many couples, simply talking about what they want to do together physically can do a lot to enhance the mood. Start there and see if it takes you any further.

If your partner makes an advance on you, but you are still not ready to have sex, try not to be harsh with your rejection. Of course, if you are not in the mood for intimacy at all, you are going to need to steer the situation in a new direction. However, if you are still feeling a little bit intimate, you can sustain the mood by taking it down a few notches. Think about things like sensual massages and petting. They might be just what you need at the moment before you feel ready to have sex. No matter what, you need to do what feels right to you. While doing your best to make your partner feel wanted, open up about how you are feeling and what you think would feel good. Great couples can compromise.

From your perspective, you might want to have sex badly, yet you are scared of being in pain from what your body has just been through. If this is the case, talk to your partner about it beforehand. While you might not be able to get back into your usual sexual routine, you can work slowly together as you build your way back up. Let your partner know if something hurts or feels uncomfortable because sex should not be either. Work together on how you can make the experience better for both of you, and you will find that you will start to crave sex more. You can use lubricants, a hot bath to loosen your muscles, and other forms of relaxation to get into the mood.

If you found that you have lost your sex drive entirely, you don't have to worry or feel bad about this. Talk to your partner, and be honest with them. They should love you unconditionally, so they will understand. After letting them know that you need a bit of time before you try again, come up with a plan together so you can both feel like you are on the same page. Make sure you let them know what types of intimacy that you are okay with and what types need to wait. Having this clarity can make the situation a lot easier for both of you. When you both have realistic expectations, neither one of you will end up feeling disappointed.

There is no right or wrong way to be intimate with your partner. As you have already established trust when you first met one another, you had to learn what you both like and dislike. In a way, having a baby is like the beginning of a brand new relationship between you two. Your body just went through a lot of physical changes, and your mind is probably emotionally different as well. You need to tell your partner what feels good and what no longer feels good, even if it is something that you used to love in the past. When you can both realize that there will be changes but they can be for the better, you will be able to feel less pressured when it comes to sharing intimacy.

Getting Back to the Old Relationship

Get rid of the idea that you are going to retreat back to your original relationship. Things are going to be different now, but that isn't a bad thing! You both have a baby to take care of, and this changes a lot in both of your lives. While you now have even more immediate responsibilities to tend to, you also have another being to consider when you make decisions. Everything that you do now impacts your baby, and this is a big role to take on—this is what it is like to be a parent. While you might never return to your impulsive and carefree relationship, you can both learn how to appreciate your new family and what you have now.

Everyone needs to evolve and grow in life; this is a positive thing. Having a baby is definitely a prime opportunity to experience this growth. It forces you to become responsible because you are no longer only impacting yourself with the decisions that you make. Even in a committed relationship, your decisions are not always going to impact your partner. When you have a baby that is relying on you for care, nearly everything that you do matters to them, even when you choose to get up and use the bathroom. Your baby needs you, especially during this infancy stage. You must make sure that you are there for them as best as you can be.

Through parenting, it is definitely possible that you become closer to your partner than ever. Just as you are working on forming a bond with your baby, a new type of bond will become present in your relationship. This one will revolve around decision-making and problem-solving, both tasks that you will become experts in as you start to raise a child together. It is a way that your relationship can grow and mature, allowing you to feel even closer to one another than you did before. Instead of thinking that the fun part of your relationship is over, look at this as the new beginning. You can still have fun together, and what you do behind closed doors is up to you. As long as you are caring for your child in the process, you do not have to give up everything that made your relationship satisfying in the past.

As a couple, you might need to rediscover one another after you have both been parents for a little while. Your priorities might change as you try to navigate through life as a parent, but this doesn't have to be a bad thing. Get on the same page with your partner, and you will both feel connected to one another. You might even surprise each other with these new priorities and new realizations. Seeing your partner in action and taking responsibility might even become one of your new turn-ons. As parents, you will each learn how to appreciate where the other is coming from because you can both relate to the decisions that must be made to raise your baby.

Many couples find that parenthood allows them to fall in love all over again. Because you are seeing your partner in a new light, you are naturally going to notice all of the things that you were originally attracted to when you first met. Learn how to appreciate these traits, and understand exactly who your partner is and what they stand for. You will probably be pretty impressed with the person that you see standing before you. Parenting isn't a perfect job, but neither is being a happy couple. Even without a baby in the picture, your relationship would have evolved in other ways. Learn how to embrace change, and know that it is happening for the best. Eventually, everything is going to fall into place and you are going to be a couple that is not only happy, but having fun.

Conclusion

You have a lot of wonderful days to look forward to as you enter this journey of motherhood. Remember that you do not need to have everything all figured out, as even veteran moms do not. What is important is listening to your baby and learning how to bond with them. Once you two have this closeness, you will be inseparable. The better you get to know one another, the better your communication will become. You would be surprised at how expressive an infant can be, even without the use of words. Your baby will know how to talk to you, through their eyes and other body movements. They will grunt, snort, and coo until you receive the message.

If you are ever second-guessing anything that you are doing as a mother, know that you have a built-in motherly instinct that will kick in. This instinct will help you make the best decisions possible, but you are not on this journey alone. Don't forget to rely on your partner for help. While they did not carry or deliver your baby, the time to level the playing field starts now. You can both take turns caring for and feeding your little one so you don't become exhausted at the same time. By keeping your relationship strong and forming a great partnership, neither one of you should feel burnt out at the thought of getting up to do another late-night feeding or to change another dirty diaper.

This stage of infancy does not last long. Before you know it, you will have a toddler who is wobbling around your home, and then a new stage will begin. Enjoy this time that you have with your newborn, and cherish all of the moments that you get to spend together. This is your chance to lay down a foundation for them that will remain with them for the rest of their life. This foundation will keep them well-organized and on the right path in life. With this kind of guidance, your baby is going to feel lucky to have you as their mother.

If you have any questions, don't be afraid to ask. There is no such thing as calling your doctor too much. This shows that your maternal instinct is strong and working well. It is much better to double-check something that you are unsure of, rather than sitting on this information and hoping that things get better. Through this book, you have learned a lot about your baby and what to expect. Between the knowledge that you have gathered here and the input from your doctor, you should have everything that you need to raise a happy and healthy baby.

Above all, don't forget to have fun! This is what parenting is all about. You are going to witness your little one experiencing new things daily, and this is a magical sight. Appreciate these moments that you get to spend together as a family, and allow them to bring you all closer together. Being a great mother does not mean being the most organized or put-together, but it does mean learning as much as you can about your baby and doing everything it takes to make them comfortable and happy, even when you feel like you can't keep on pushing anymore. Thank you for reading this book and allowing it to guide you through your first moments of motherhood! Please leave a favorable reply. You are a superhero that should be celebrated! Wear your 'mom' title proud, and remember that you can do anything you set your mind to.

References

"5 Signs Your Baby Has a Fever." Nurofen Australia, 24 Apr. 2017, www.nurofen.com.au/pain-advice/fever/5-signs-your-baby-has-a-fever/.

Bjarnadottir, A. (2017, June 1). *Breastfeeding Diet 101 - What to Eat While Breastfeeding.* Retrieved from https://www.healthline.com/nutrition/breastfeeding-diet-101#section3

Breastfeeding Checklist. (n.d.). Retrieved from https://newmothernewbaby.com/pages/checklist.html

Breastmilk. Every Ounce Counts. (n.d.). Retrieved from https://www.breastmilkcounts.com/breastfeeding-101/skin-to-skin/#:~:text=The Benefits of Skin-to-Skin&text=Calms you and baby.,mom's stress and promotes healing.

Boulanger, A. (2014, November 6). *Infant and Toddler Vaccine Schedule.* Retrieved from https://www.healthline.com/health/vaccinations/infant-immunization-schedule#vaccine-descriptions

Brennan, D. (2019, June 25). *Mastitis: Symptoms (Fever After Breastfeeding), Treatment & Prevention.*

Retrieved   from
https://www.webmd.com/parenting/baby/wh
at-is-mastitis#1

Brimdyr, K. (n.d.). *The Magical Hour.* Retrieved from
http://www.magicalhour.org/aboutus.html

Cappetta, K. (2017, July 27). *13 Best Labor and Birthing
Positions.*   Retrieved   from
https://www.thebump.com/a/birthing-
positions

Cassar-Uhl, D. (2018, March 27). *Hypoplasia/Insufficient
Glandular Tissue* • KellyMom.com. Retrieved
from   https://kellymom.com/bf/got-
milk/supply-worries/insufficient-glandular-
tissue/

Crouch, M. (2019, June 9). 39 *Breastfeeding Secrets Every
New Mother Should Know.* Retrieved from
https://www.parents.com/baby/breastfeeding/
tips/31-breastfeeding-secrets/

DesMarais, C. (2019, September 28). *Science Says the Most
Successful Kids Have Parents Who Do These 5 Things.*
Retrieved from https://www.inc.com/christina-
desmarais/science-says-most-successful-kids-
have-parents-who-do-these-5-things_2.html

Conte, K. *"Baby Skin Issues and Conditions."* What to
Expect, WhattoExpect, 26 Nov. 2018,
www.whattoexpect.com/first-year/health-and-
safety/baby-skin-issues-conditions/

"Ear Infections 101: Commonly Asked Questions For Parents." *Ear Infections 101: Commonly Asked Questions For Parents* | Texas Children's Hospital, 8 Oct. 2014, www.texaschildrens.org/blog/2014/10/ear-infections-101-commonly-asked-questions-parents.

Fischer, K. (2019, April 5). *C-Section Benefits.* Retrieved from https://www.healthline.com/health-news/some-benefits-to-c-sections-researchers-say#2

Gagne, C. (2020, April 21). *Get ready to Netflix and sleep, parents! 5 steps to getting your baby on a sleep schedule.* Retrieved from https://www.todaysparent.com/baby/baby-sleep/steps-to-get-your-baby-on-a-sleep-schedule/

Homepage. (2020, April 29). Retrieved from https://www.llli.org/

Keeping breast milk safe and healthy. (2019, March). Retrieved from https://www.marchofdimes.org/baby/keeping-breast-milk-safe-and-healthy.aspx#:~:text=Most over-the-counter (,safe to use when breastfeeding.

Marcoux, H. (2020, June 5). *85% of moms dont think society understands or supports motherhood.* Retrieved from https://www.mother.ly/news/the-2019-state-

of-motherhood-survey-millennial-mothers-
need-support

Masters, M. (2018, November 21). *12 Ways to Soothe a Crying Baby*. Retrieved from https://www.whattoexpect.com/first-year/photo-gallery/soothing-a-crying-baby.aspx

Masters, M. (2019, July 10). *What Is a Doula and Should You Hire One for Your Baby's Birth?* Retrieved from https://www.whattoexpect.com/pregnancy/hiring-doula#:~:text=Studies have shown that doulas,-baby bonding post-birth.

Murray, D. (2020, March 7). *How Mothers Can Keep Leaky Breasts Under Control*. Retrieved from https://www.verywellfamily.com/leaking-breast-milk-431582

Nair, A. (2020, April 6). *15 Most Common Infants & Newborn Problems and Diseases*. Retrieved from https://parenting.firstcry.com/articles/15-common-baby-problems-and-diseases/

Northwestern Medicine. (n.d.). *Newborn Hygiene*. Retrieved from https://www.nm.org/conditions-and-care-areas/pediatrics/pediatric-infant-and-newborn-care/hygiene

Osmond, C. (2020, May 22). *The Pros and Cons of Co-Sleeping*. Retrieved from https://www.thesleepjudge.com/pros-and-cons-of-co-sleeping/

Pampers. (2019, April 11). *What to Include in Your Birth Plan.* Retrieved from https://www.pampers.com/en-us/pregnancy/giving-birth/article/what-to-include-in-your-birth-plan

Reyes, K. (2016, December 11). *Pregnancy, Parenting, Lifestyle, Beauty: Tips & Advice.* Retrieved from https://mom.com/baby/38021-things-moms-worry-about-most

Smith, M, and J Segal. *"Postpartum Depression and the Baby Blues."* HelpGuide.org, Oct. 2019, www.helpguide.org/articles/depression/postpartum-depression-and-the-baby-blues.htm.

Springen, K, et al. *"How to Soothe a Colicky Baby."* Parents, 9 Jan. 2020, www.parents.com/baby/care/colic/how-to-soothe-a-colicky-baby/.

Tatar, E. (2016, April 20). *Breast milk vs. formula: What do the studies really tell us?* Retrieved from https://www.inquirer.com/philly/blogs/healthy_kids/Breast-milk-vs-formula-What-do-the-studies-really-tell-us.html

Teaching Your Baby to Put Himself to Sleep. (n.d.). Retrieved from https://www.ahaparenting.com/Ages-

stages/babies/teaching-your-baby-to-put-
himself-to-sleep

Underwood, P. (2020, April 17). *Yes, You Absolutely Need
to Baby Proof.* Retrieved from
https://www.nytimes.com/article/babyproofin
g-guide.html

"Vomiting in Children and Babies." NHS Inform, 14 Feb.
2020, www.nhsinform.scot/illnesses-and-
conditions/stomach-liver-and-gastrointestinal-
tract/vomiting-in-children-and-babies.

Made in the USA
Monee, IL
19 July 2021

73909308R00085